Peoples of the Steppe

Historical Sources on the Pastoral Nomads of Eurasia

David C. Wright

Brigham Young University

SIMON & SCHUSTER

Cover art: "Chingiz Khan riding into battle," Courtesy of Bibliotheque Nationale, Paris, France

Printed in the United States of America

10 9 8 7 6 5 4 3 2 1

Please visit our website at www.sscp.com

ISBN 0–536–01467–1

BA 98338

SIMON & SCHUSTER PUBLISHING
160 Gould Street/Needham Heights, MA 02494
Simon & Schuster Education Group

COPYRIGHT ACKNOWLEDGMENTS

Grateful acknowledgment is made to the following sources for permission to reprint material copyrighted or controlled by them:

"Preface and Introduction," by Rene Grousset, reprinted from *The Empire of the Steppes: A History of Central Asia*, translated by Naomi Walford, 1970, by permission of Rutgers University Press. Copyright © 1970 by Rutgers, The State University of New Jersey.

"Introduction the Phenomenon of Nomadism: Myths and Problems," excerpt from Chapter 1, "Nomadism as a Distinct Form of Food-Producing Economy," by A. M. Khazanov, reprinted from *Nomads and the Outside World*, 1983, Cambridge University Press. Copyright © 1983 by Cambridge University Press.

Excerpts from "Book Four," by Herodotus, reprinted from *Herodotus: The Histories*, translated by Aubrey de Selincourt, 1954, Penguin Books, Ltd.

Excerpts from "Shih chi 110: The Account of the Hsiung-nu," by Ssu-Ma Ch'ien, reprinted from *Records of the Grand Historian of China, Volume II: The Age of Emperor Wu 140 to circa 100 B.C.*, translated by Burton Watson, 1968, by permission of Columbia University Press. Copyright © 1961 by Columbia University.

Excerpts from "Book 31," by Ammianus Marcellinus, reprinted from *The Later Roman Empire (A.D. 354-378)*, translated by Walter Hamilton, 1986, Penguin Books, Ltd.

"Excerpts," by Isidore de Seville, reprinted from *Isidore of Seville's History of the Goths, Vandals, and Suevi*, translated by Guido Donini and Gordon B. Ford, Jr., 1970, EJ Brill USA, Inc.

"Excerpts," by Jordanes, reprinted from *The Gothic History of Jordanes*, translated by Charles Christopher Mierow, Ph.D., 1915, Princeton University Press.

Excerpts from "Turko-Scythian Tribes—After Han Dynasty," translated by E. W. Parker, reprinted from *The China Review of Notes and Queries on the Far East*, Vol. XX, 1892–1893.

Excerpts from "The Early Turks," translated by E.W. Parker, reprinted from *The China Review or Notes and Queries on the Far East*, Vol. XXIV, No. 1, December and January 1900.

Excerpts from "The Early Turks," translated by E.W. Parker, reprinted from *The China Review or Notes and Queries on the Far East*, Vol. XXIV, No. 5, April and May, 1900.

"Excerpts," edited and translated by Colin Mackerras, reprinted from *The Uighur Empire: According to the T'ang Dynastic Histories, A Study in Sino-Uighur Relations 744-840*, 1972, Australian National University Press.

"Excerpts from The Early Turks - Part V," translated by E.W. Parker, reprinted from *The China Review or Notes and Queries on the Far East*, Vol. XXV, No. VI, June and July 1901.

"Excerpts," by Ibn Al-Athir; Bertold Spuler, reprinted from *History of the Mongols: Based on Eastern and Western Accounts of the Thirteenth and Fourteenth Centuries*, translated by Helga and Stuart Drummond, 1968, University of California Press.

"Excerpts," by Ch'iu Ch'u-chi, reprinted from *Medieval Researches from Eastern Asiatic Sources: Fragments Towards the Knowledge of the Geography and History of Central and Western Asia From the 13th to the 17th Century*, translated by E. Bretschneider, M.D., 1910, Kegan Paul, Trench, Trubner & Co. Ltd.

"Excerpts," by John of Plano Carpini, reprinted from *The Mongol Mission: Narratives and Letters of the Franciscan Missionaries in Mongolia and China in the Thirteenth and Fourteenth Centuries*, edited by Christopher Dawson, 1955, Sheed & Ward, Inc.

"Guyuk Khan's Letter to Pope Innocent IV (1246)," by Guyuk Khan, reprinted from *The Mongol Mission: Narratives and Letters of the Franciscan Missionaries in Mongolia and China in the Thirteenth and Fourteenth Centuries*, edited by Christopher Dawson, 1955, Sheed & Ward, Inc.

Excerpts from "The Journey of William of Rubruck," by William of Rubruck, reprinted from *The Mongol Mission: Narratives and Letters of the Franciscan Missionaries in Mongolia and China in the Thirteenth and Fourteenth Centuries*, edited by Christopher Dawson, 1955, Sheed & Ward, Inc.

Excerpts from "Of the Condition of the Mongols Before the Time of Chingiz-Khan's Rise to Power," by Ala-ad-Din Ata-Malik Juvaini, reprinted from *Genghis Khan: The History of the World-Conquerer*, translated by John A. Boyle, Ph.D., 1958, Manchester University Press.

Excerpts from "The Ilkhan Dynasty in Persia (1256-1335/54)," by Wassaf al-Hadrat, reprinted from *History of the Mongols: Based on Eastern and Western Accounts of the Thirteenth and Fourteenth Centuries*, translated by Bertold Spuler (German), and Helga and Stuart Drummond, 1968, Routledge.

Excerpts from "The Travels of Marco Polo," by Marco Polo, reprinted from *The Book of Ser Marco Polo the Venetian Concerning the Kingdoms and Marvels of the East*, translated by Henry Yule, 1903, John Murray.

CONTENTS

And Abel was a keeper of sheep, but Cain was a tiller of the ground.

Genesis 4:2

Lo, I will bring a nation upon you from afar, O house of Israel, saith the LORD: It is a mighty nation, it is an ancient nation, a nation whose language thou knowest not, neither understandest what they say. Their quiver is as an open sepulchre, they are all mighty men. And they shall eat up shine harvest, and thy bread, which thy sons and thy daughters should eat: they shall eat up thy flocks and thine herds: they shall eat up thy vines and thy fig trees: they shall impoverish thy fenced cities, wherein thou trustedst, with the sword.

Jeremiah 5: 15–17

Introduction

This volume is a "nomad reader." That is, it contains historical reading material on the *pastoral nomads*, peoples whose ecology involved not primarily hunting and gathering on the one hand or sedentary agricultural activity on the other, but rather the domestication of animals (pastoralism) and continual human movement along with the animals in search of naturally occurring pasturage (nomadism). Nomads seldom were literate and thus almost never maintained their own written historical records, so historians today must rely on the writings of historians of Rome, Greece, Persia, China, and other sedentary civilizations for information. This volume contains two secondary studies by prominent twentieth-century scholars who have studied the history of the pastoral nomads, but the bulk of the readings are by pre-modern writers and historians. My hope is that these texts will speak for themselves.

Some of the texts contain material that will undoubtedly be unfamiliar to most students. My hope is that the fine detail of the accounts will not overwhelm the student; it is certainly not my intent to require memorization or digestion of large amounts of historical trivia. After each reading I have included some reading questions, and students may consider these questions conceptual compasses with which to navigate their ways through these sometimes complex and involved texts. I hope students will relax and have some fun with these accounts; they are, after all, records about real and exciting human events in the past.

I owe the initial idea for the inception of this volume to my friend and colleague Professor David C. Montgomery of Brigham Young University. David has been a superb teacher, mentor, and colleague to me for over a decade now. I also owe thanks to Prof. Sechin Jagchid for initially piquing my interest in the pastoral nomads and the problem of their historical interaction with civilized societies. While I no longer agree with some of Sechin's perspectives on the history of interaction between the steppe and the civilized world,[1] I am nonetheless in his debt for his patient interest in my scholarship over the years.

I thank my colleague William J. Hamblin for producing the handsome map of the steppe or grassland region of the Eurasian landmass, the region historically inhabited by the pastoral nomads.

David C. Wright
Provo and Orem, Utah
May 1998

---

[1]See my review article "Wealth and War in Sino-Nomadic Relations" in *Tsing Hua Journal of Chinese Studies* 25.3 (Sept. 1995): 295–308.

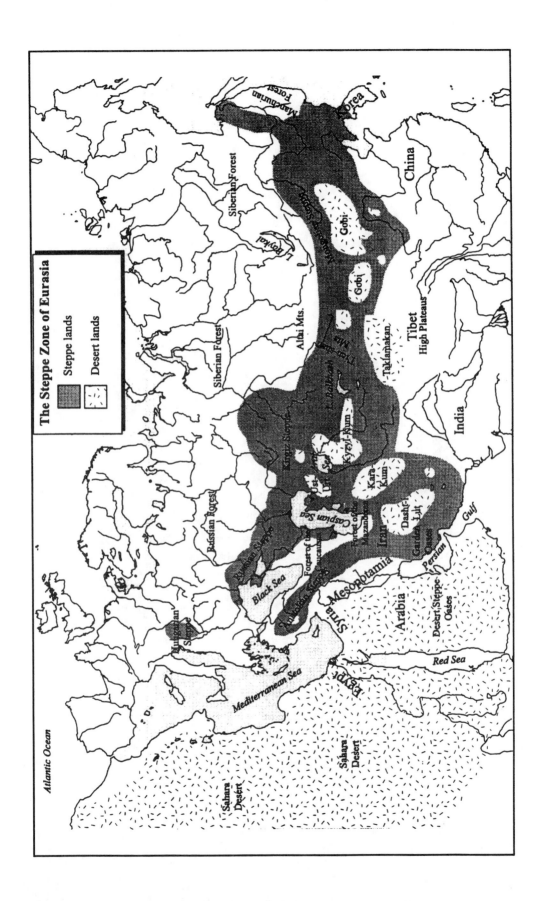

The Steppe Zone of Eurasia

Steppe lands

Desert lands

Atlantic Ocean

Siberian Forest

Siberian Forest

Russian Forest

L. Baykal

Altai Mts.

Manchurian Forest

Korea

China

Gobi

Gobi

Taklamakan

Tibet
High Plateaus

India

Kazak Steppe

Kirgiz Steppe

Russian Steppe

Ukrainian Steppe

Black Sea

Ust Urt

Aral Sea

Kyzyl-Kum

L. Balkhash

Kara-Kum

Caspian Sea

Dasht-i-Lut
Garden
Oases

Iran

Mazanderan
Forest

Forest of Gilan

Persian Gulf

Gulf

Mesopotamia

Syria

Egypt

Arabia

Desert;Steppe
Oasis

Red Sea

Mediterranean Sea

Sahara
Desert

Sahara
Desert

I.

Modern Scholarship
on the Pastoral Nomads

A. Grousset

I n the West, the great French Orientalist René Grousset
(1885–1952) is likely the best known of twentieth-century scholars
of the history of the pastoral nomads and their interaction with
sedentary civilizations. Grousset was somewhat acquainted with
"Oriental" or Asian languages, but his greatest and most enduring
contribution was his ability to digest dense, highly technical
monographs by other European scholars and condense them into the
effortlessly limpid prose for which the French are justly famous. The
most notable of his works is his monumental *L'Empire des Steppes*,
first published in 1939 and translated into English in 1970 *as The
Empire of the Steppe: A History of Central Asia*. This book is nothing less
than a comprehensive survey of steppe history, from the Scythians
known to the ancient Greeks to the last hurrah of nomadic power on
the frontiers of eighteenth-century China. Deborah Amos of National
Public Radio once asked me to recommend a single book on the
history of Central Asia, and I unhesitatingly told her about
Grousset's masterwork. And I now commend the following excerpts
from it to my students.

The Empire of the Steppes
A History of Central Asia

René Grousset

Preface

Attila, Jenghiz Khan, Tamerlane: their names are in everyone's memory. Accounts of them written by western chroniclers and by Chinese or Persian annalists have served to spread their repute. The great barbarians irrupt into areas of developed historical civilizations and suddenly, within a few years, reduce the Roman, Iranian, or Chinese world to a heap of ruins. Their arrival, motives, and disappearance seem inexplicable, so much so that historians today come near to adopting the verdict of the writers of old, who saw in them the scourge of the Lord, sent for the chastisement of ancient civilizations.

Yet never were men more sons of the earth than these, more the natural product of their environment; but their motivations and patterns of behavior acquire clarity as we come to understand their way of life. These stunted, stocky bodies—invincible, since they could survive such rigorous conditions—were formed by the steppes. The bitter winds of the high plateaus, the intense cold and torrid heat, carved those faces with their wrinkled eyes, high cheekbones, and sparse hair, and hardened those sinewy frames. The demands of a pastoral life, governed by seasonal migrations in search of pasture, defined their specific nomadism, and the exigencies of their nomadic economy determined their relations with sedentary peoples: relations consisting by turns of timid borrowings and bloodthirsty raids.

The three or four great Asiatic nomads who burst upon us to rip up the web of history seem to us exceptional solely because of our own ignorance. For three who achieved the astounding feat of becoming conquerors of the world, how many Attilas and Jenghiz Khans have failed? Failed, that is, to do more than found limited empires comprising a quarter of Asia, from Siberia to the Yellow River, from the Altai to Persia—an achievement which one must nevertheless acknowledge to have been of some magnitude. I would like to bring before your minds this great barbarian people, dominated by three mighty figures—Attila, Jenghiz Khan, Tamerlane—as they march through ten centuries of history, from the borders of China to the frontiers of the West.

The problem of the barbarians must be stated precisely. The classical world encountered many kinds of barbarians, that is, people so designated by their neighbors. The Celts were barbarians to the Romans for a long time, as were the Germans to Gaul, and the Slav world to Germania. Similarly, the land afterward known as southern China long remained a barbarian country to the original Chinese of the Yellow River. But because geographical conditions in all these regions imposed an agricultural way of life upon their inhabitants, they emerged from their backwardness to become increasingly identified with that life, so that by the second half of the Middle Ages almost the whole of Europe, Western Asia, Iran, the Indies, and China had attained the same stage of material civilization.

Yet one important area escaped this process—the wide belt stretching across the northern part of Central Eurasia from the borders of Manchuria to Budapest. This is the steppe zone, penetrated along its northern edges by the Siberian forest. Geographical conditions here allowed only a few patches of cultivation, so that the inhabitants were forced to follow a pastoral, nomadic way of life, such as the rest of humanity had known thousands of years earlier at the end of the Neolithic age. Indeed, some of these tribes—those of the forest zone—remained at the cultural stage of the Magdalenian hunters. Thus the steppe and forest region remained a preserve of barbarism—not, be it understood, in the sense that the people living there were inferior as human beings to the rest of mankind, but because local conditions perpetuated a way of life which elsewhere had long since passed away.

The survival of these pastoral peoples into an era when the rest of Asia had arrived at an advanced agricultural stage was a very important factor in the drama of history. It involved a sort of time shift between neighboring peoples. Men of the second millennium B.C. coexisted with those of the twelfth century A.D. To pass from one group to the other, one had only to come down from Upper Mongolia to Peking, or to climb from the Kirghiz steppe to Ispahan. The break was abrupt and fraught with perils. To the sedentary peoples of China, Iran, and Europe, the Hun, the Turkoman, and the Mongol were savages indeed, to be intimidated by a display of arms, amused by glass beads and by titles, and kept at a respectful distance from cultivated land. The attitude of the nomads may be easily imagined. The poor Turko-Mongol herdsmen who in years of drought ventured across the meager grazing of the steppe from one dried-up waterhole to another, to the very fringe of cultivation, at the gates of Pechili (Hopei) or Transoxiana, gazed thunderstruck at the miracle of sedentary civilization: luxuriant crops, villages crammed with grain, and the luxury of the towns. This miracle, or rather its secret—the patient toil required to maintain these human hives— was beyond the comprehension of the Hun. If he was fascinated, it was like the wolf—his totem—when in snowy weather it draws near to the farms and spies its prey within the wattled fence. He too had the age-old impulse to break in, plunder, and escape with his booty.

The survival of a herding and hunting community beside a farming one—or, put differently, the development of increasingly prosperous agricultural communities within sight and contact of peoples still at the pastoral stage, and suffering the appalling famines inherent in steppe life in time of drought—presented not only a glaring economic contrast but a social contrast that was even crueler. To repeat, the problem of human geography became a social one. The attitudes of the sedentary man and the nomad toward each other recall the feelings of a capitalist society and a proletariat enclosed within a modern city. The farming communities that cultivated the good yellow soil of northern China, the gardens of Iran, or the rich black earth of Kiev were encircled by a belt of poor grazing land where terrible climatic conditions often prevailed, and where one year in every ten the watering places dried up, grass withered, and livestock perished, and with them the nomad himself.

In these circumstances, the periodic thrusts of the nomads into the cultivated areas were a law of nature. It should be added that whether Turks or Mongols, they belonged to an intelligent, levelheaded, practical people which, drilled by the harsh realities of its environment, was ever ready for the word of command. When the sedentary and often decadent communities yielded under his onslaught, the nomad entered the city and, when the first few hours of massacre were over, without any great difficulty took the place of the rulers whom he had defeated. Unabashed, he seated himself upon the most time-honored and exalted thrones, as grand khan of

China, king of Persia, emperor of India, or sultan of Rum, and adapted himself accordingly. In Peking he became half Chinese, in Ispahan or Rai half Persian.

Was that the final outcome—a permanent reconciliation between the steppe and the town? By no means. The inexorable laws of human geography continued to operate. If the Sinicized or Iranized khan was not removed by some native reaction, whether slow or sudden, from the depths of the steppes new hordes, and hungry ones, would appear at his frontiers, and seeing in their upstart cousin merely another Tadzhik or Tabgatch—Persian or Chinese—repeat the adventure, to his disadvantage.

How is it that the adventure was nearly always successful, and that the same rhythm recurred throughout thirteen centuries—that period between the Huns' entry into Loyang and the Manchus' into Peking? The answer is that the nomad, retarded though he was in material culture, always possessed a tremendous military ascendancy. He was the mounted archer. The technical arm, which gave him almost as great an advantage over sedentary man as artillery gave modern Europe over the rest of the world, was an incredibly mobile cavalry of expert bowmen. It is true that neither Chinese nor Iranians neglected this arm. From the third century B.C. on, the Chinese adapted their dress for riding. And Persia, from the times of the Parthians, knew the value of a shower of arrows delivered by a whirl of retreating horsemen. But Chinese, Iranian, Russian, Pole, or Hungarian could never equal the Mongol in this field. Trained from childhood to drive deer at a gallop over the vast expanses of the steppe, accustomed to patient stalking and to all the ruses of the hunter on which his food—that is, his life—depended, he was unbeatable. Not that he often confronted his enemy; on the contrary, having launched a surprise attack upon him, he would vanish; reappear, pursue him ardently without letting himself be caught, harry him, weary him, and at last bring him down exhausted, like driven game. The deceptive mobility and ubiquity of this cavalry, when handled by a Jebe or a Sübötäi—Jenghiz Khan's two great generals—endowed this arm with a sort of corporate intelligence. Piano Carpini and Rubruck, who watched it in action, were much struck by this decisive technical superiority. The phalanx and the legion passed away because they had been born of the political constitutions of Macedonia and Rome; they were the planned creation of organized states which, like all states, arose, lived, and disappeared. The mounted archer of the steppe reigned over Eurasia for thirteen centuries because he was the spontaneous creation of the soil itself: the offspring of hunger and want, the nomads' only means of survival during years of famine. When Jenghiz Khan succeeded in conquering the world, he was able to do so because, as an orphan abandoned on the plain of Kerulen, he had already succeeded, with his young brother Jöchi the Tiger, in bringing down enough game daily to escape death by starvation.

The arrow of the mounted archer who dashed in, let fly, and fled was for antiquity and the Middle Ages a form of indirect fire, almost as effective and demoralizing in its time as that of the gunners of today.

What put an end to this superiority? How is it that starting in the sixteenth century the nomad no longer had the sedentary peoples at his mercy? The reason was that the latter now met him with artillery, and thus overnight acquired an artificial ascendancy over him. An agelong position was reversed. The cannonades with which Ivan the Terrible scattered the last heirs of the Golden Horde, and with which the K'ang-hsi emperor of China frightened the Kalmucks, marked the end of a period of world history. For the first time, and for ever, military technique had changed camps and civilization became stronger than barbarism. Within a few hours the traditional superiority of the nomad faded into a seemingly unreal past, and the Kalmuck archers whom the romantic Czar Alexander I marshaled against Napoleon on the battlefields of 1807 were to appear as out of date as Magdalenian hunters.

Yet only three centuries had passed since those archers ceased to be conquerors of the world.

Introduction: The Steppe and History

In their physical manifestation, the high plateaus of Asia bear witness to the most tremendous geological drama in the history of this planet. The upheaval and isolation of this huge continental mass were due to the converging assaults of two great chains of folded mountains formed in two different periods: the Hercynian folds of the T'ien Shan and Altai ranges—the first of these being bordered by the Serindian mass and the second by the ancient Siberian plateau of Angaraland—and the Himalayan alpine folds, which in the Miocene period replaced the ancient "Mediterranean" Sea of Eurasia. The arc of the T'ien Shan and Altai to the northwest, and the opposing curve of the Himalayas in the south, together encircle and isolate Turkestan and Mongolia, leaving them, as it were, suspended above the surrounding plains. Because of their altitude and their great distance from the sea, these regions experience a continental climate of great extremes, with excessive heat in summer and bitter cold in winter. At Urga (Ulan Bator), in Mongolia, the temperature varies from +38° to –42° Centigrade. With the exception of the Tibetan massif, the great altitude of which produces almost polar vegetation, and also of the semicircular ranges of the Altai and T'ien Shan, which, for similar reasons, have an alpine climate characteristically graded from the forests of the foothills to the sparse vegetation on the peaks, almost the whole of continental Asia is covered by a longitudinal belt of grassy steppes, dormant in winter and dried up in summer. The prairie steppes—fertile in their irrigated areas, but shriveling and turning into desert in the central wastes—run from Manchuria to the Crimea, from Urga in Outer Mongolia to the regions of Merv and Balkh, where the North Eurasian prairie steppe gives place to the dry, subtropical steppe, more Mediterranean in character, of Iran and Afghanistan.

To the north, the longitudinal belt of the Eurasian steppes merges with the boreal forest region of central Russia and Siberia, and with the northern fringe of Mongolia and Manchuria. In three areas in the middle of the belt, the steppe imperceptibly yields to the desert: the deserts of Kyzyl-Kum in Transoxiana and Kara-Kum south of the Amu Darya; the desert of Taklamakan in the enclosed Tarim basin; and lastly the Gobi Desert, a vast area stretching from southwest to northeast, from the Lob Nor, where the Gobi joins the Taklamakan, to the Khingan Mountains on the borders of Manchuria. They are like cancerous patches devouring the grassy belt, on which they have been continually encroaching since protohistoric times. The situation of the Gobi Desert, lying as it does between northern Mongolia, the forests of Baikal, and the steppes of the Orkhon and Kerulen to the north and southern Mongolia and the steppes of Alashan, Ordos, Chahar, and Jehol to the south, is one of the enduring factors preventing the survival of Turko-Mongol empires, whether of the Hsiung-nu of antiquity or of the T'u-chüeh of the Middle Ages.

This rout of the steppe by the desert gave a particularly decisive turn to the history of the Tarim basin, in what is now Chinese Turkestan. Having escaped the nomadic life of the plains (though always threatened or dominated by the northern hordes), this area acquired the urban, commercial character of the oases of the caravan routes and, by the chain of these oases, formed a line of communication between the great sedentary civilizations of the West—those of the Mediterranean world, of Iran, and of India—and that of the Far East, namely, China. A double trail was laid in a double curve north and south of the dying Tarim River: the northern route ran through Tunhwang, Hami, Turfan, Kara Shahr, Kucha, Kashgar, the Fergana basin, and Transoxiana; the southern, by way of Tunhwang, Khotan, Yarkand, the Pamir valleys, and Bactria. This slender dual thread that crosses deserts and peaks by turns, frail as a winding, long-drawn-out line of ants moving cross-country, was strong enough nevertheless to ensure that our planet should consist of a single world and not of two separate ones, and to maintain a minimum degree of contact between the anthill of China and the Indo-European anthills. It was the Silk Road and the road of pilgrimage, along which traveled trade and religion, the Greek art of Alexander's successors and Buddhist missionaries from Afghanistan. By this route the Greco-Roman merchants mentioned by Ptolemy struggled to obtain access to the bales of silk from "Serica," and Chinese generals of the second Han dynasty sought to establish communication with the Iranian world and the Roman Orient. The maintenance of this great route of world commerce was, from the Han to Kublai Khan, an age-long principle of Chinese policy.

North of this narrow trail of civilization, however, the steppes provided the nomads with a route of a very different order: a boundless route of numberless tracks, the route of barbarism. Nothing halted the thundering barbarian squadrons between the banks of the Orkhon or the Kerulen and Lake Balkhash; for, although toward the latter point the Altai Mountains and the northern spurs of the T'ien Shan ranges seem to meet, the gap is still wide at the Imil River in Tarbagatai, in the direction of Chuguchak, as also between the Yulduz, the Ili, and the Issyk Kul basin to the northwest, where the horsemen from Mongolia beheld the further boundless expanses of the Kirghiz and Russian steppes. The passes of Tarbagatai, Ala-Tau, and Muzart were continually crossed by hordes from the eastern steppe on their way to the steppes of the west. In the protohistoric period, the movement must have been more often in the opposite direction; one gains the impression that nomads of Iranian—that is, Indo-European—stock, called Scythians and Sarmatians by Greek historians and identified as Saka by Iranian inscriptions, must have penetrated a long way to the northeast, to the region of Pazyryk and Minusinsk, while other Indo-Europeans populated the Tarim oases, from Kashgar to Kucha, Kara Shahr, and Turfan, perhaps even as far as Kansu. It is certain, however, that from the beginning of the Christian era the flow was from east to west. It was no longer the Indo-European dialects that prevailed—"East Iranian," Kuchean, or Tokharian—in the oases of the future Chinese Turkestan; it was rather the Hsiung-nu who, under the name of Huns, came to establish a proto-Turkic empire in southern Russia and in Hungary. (The Hungarian steppe is a continuation of the Russian steppe, as the Russian steppe is of the Asian.) After the Huns came the Avars, a Mongol horde which had fled from Central Asia under pressure from the T'u-chüeh in the sixth century, and which was to dominate the same regions, first Russia and later Hungary. In the seventh century came the Khazar Turks, in the eleventh the Petcheneg Turks, and in the twelfth the Cuman Turks, all following the same trail. Lastly, in the thirteenth century, the Mongols of Jenghiz Khan integrated the steppe, so to speak, and became the steppe incarnate, from Peking to Kiev.

The interior history of the steppe is that of Turko-Mongol hordes jostling one another for the best grazing grounds, and of their endless migrations from pasture to pasture, driven mainly by the needs of their herds. In some instances these alternating movements took centuries to complete owing to the vast distances involved, to which everything about these people—their physical build and their way of life—had become adapted. Of these unceasing wanderings between the Yellow River and Budapest, history, written by men of sedentary nations, has retained but little, and then only such events as affected themselves. They noted the onslaught of the waves that broke at the foot of the Great Wall or of their Danubian fortresses, Tatung or Silistra. But what do they tell of the inner turbulence of the Turko-Mongol peoples? In what may be termed the imperial district of Karabalgasun and Karakorum in northern Mongolia, at the source of the Orkhon, we find all the nomad clans which aimed at the domination of other hordes: there are the Hsiung-nu, of Turkic stock, before our own era; the Mongol Hsien-pi in the third century A.D.; the Juan-juan, also Mongol, in the fifth century; T'u-chüeh Turks in the sixth; Uigur Turks in the eighth; Kirghiz in the ninth; the Khitan of Mongol stock in the tenth; the Kerayit or Naiman, presumably Turkic, in the twelfth; and lastly, in the thirteenth century, the Mongols of Jenghiz Khan. Yet although we may be able to identify these alternately Turkic and Mongol clans which imposed their hegemony on others, we do not know how the great parent groups, Turkic, Mongol, and Tungus, were originally distributed. No doubt at the present time the Tungus occupy not only northern Manchuria but a great part of eastern Siberia, as well as the east bank of the middle Yenisei in central Siberia; while the Mongols are grouped in historic Mongolia and the Turks in western Siberia and the two Turkestans. It should be remembered, however, that in this latter region the Turks are latecomers and that their influence in the Altai may not have made itself felt until the first century of our era, in Kashgaria certainly not before the ninth century, and in Transoxiana not before the eleventh. The urban population both in Samarkand and Kashgar remains fundamentally of Turkicized Iranian stock. Nevertheless, history tells that in Mongolia itself the Jenghiz-Khanites Mongolized many apparently Turkic tribes: the Naiman of the Altai, the Kerayit of the Gobi, and the Öngüt of Chahar. Before the unification under Jenghiz Khan which brought all these tribes under the banner of the Blue Mongols, part of present-day Mongolia was Turkic; indeed, even now a Turkic people, the Yakut, occupy northeastern Siberia, north of the Tungus, in the Lena, Indigirka, and Kolyma basins. The presence of this Turkic group so near Bering Strait, north of the Mongols and even of the Tungus on the Arctic Ocean, necessitates caution in attempts to determine the relative positions of the "first" Turks, Mongols, and Tungus. What it does indicate is that the Turko-Mongol and Tungus mass must originally have been established fairly far to the northeast; for not only present-day Kashgaria but also the northern slopes of the Sayan Mountains (Minusinsk) and the Great Altai (Pazyryk) were at that time peopled by Indo-Europeans from the "common Indo-European" cradle of southern Russia. Such a hypothesis is consistent with the views of such linguists as Pelliot and Guillaume de Hévésy, who, until further evidence is forthcoming, refuse to entertain any original connection between the Altaic languages (Turkic, Mongol, and Tungus) and those of the Finno-Ugrian group, centered in the Urals. Moreover, the fairly wide divergence existing today, despite their original kinship, between Turkic, Mongol, and Tungus leads us to think that the three groups which during the historic period were united under common rule (hence frequent reciprocal borrowings of terms of civilization) may for a time have existed at some distance from each other, across the vastness of the Asian northeast.

Were the history of the Turko-Mongol hordes confined to their expeditions and obscure skirmishes in the search for new pastures, it would amount to very little, at least as far as present interest is concerned. The paramount fact in human history is the pressure exerted by these nomads on the civilized empires of the south, a pressure constantly repeated until conquest was achieved. The descent of the nomads amounted almost to a physical law, dictated by the conditions prevailing in their native steppes.

Certainly, those Turko-Mongols who remained in the forest region of Lake Baikal and the Amur continued to be savages, and lived by hunting and fishing, as did the Jurchid down to the twelfth century and the "Forest Mongols" until the time of Jenghiz Khan; they were too closely barricaded by their wooded solitudes to conceive of other covetable territories. It was otherwise with the Turko-Mongols of the steppes, who lived by their herds and who were therefore nomads by necessity: the herd sought grass and they followed the herd.

Added to this, the steppe is the land of the horse. The man of the steppe is a horseman born. Whether an Iranian of the west or a Turko-Mongol of the east, it was he who invented the riding dress, such as we see worn by the Scythians portrayed on Greek vases of the Cimmerian Bosporus, and hear of from the Chinese, who, in 300 B.C., to fight cavalry with cavalry, imitated the Huns in substituting trousers for robes. The horseman of the lightning raids was a mounted archer who brought down his adversary from a distance, shot while retreating—the Parthian shaft is in fact that of the Scythian and the Hun—and waged war as he pursued game or mares: with arrow and lasso.

On the threshold of these forays, where the steppes ended and cultivation began, he glimpsed a way of life very different from his own, one which was bound to arouse his greed. Winter on his native steppe is arctic; the steppe at that season is an extension of the Siberian taiga. Summer is scorching, for then the steppe is a continuation of the Gobi Desert, and to find pasture for his herds the nomad must climb the slopes of the Khingan, Altai, or Tarbagatai ranges. Spring alone, which transforms the steppe into a lush plain, strewn with flowers of every color, was a festival season for his beasts and for himself. Throughout the rest of the year, and especially in winter, his eyes were turned toward the temperate lands of the south, to Issyk Kul, "the hot lake" in the southwest, to the good yellow lands of the Yellow River in the southeast. Not that he had any taste for cultivated land as such; when he took possession of it, he instinctively allowed it to relapse into a fallow, unproductive state, and fields reverted to steppe, to yield grass for his sheep and horses.

Such was the attitude of Jenghiz Khan in the thirteenth century. Having conquered the Peking region, his genuine desire was to raise the millet fields of the fair plain of Hopei to the dignity of grazing land. Yet, although the man from the north understood nothing of husbandry (until the fourteenth century the Jenghiz-Khanites of Turkestan and Russia remained pure nomads, foolishly sacking their own towns and—at the least refusal to pay up on the part of the farmers—diverting irrigation canals to starve the land), he appreciated urban civilizations for their manufactured goods and their many amenities, as objects of sack and plunder. He was attracted by the mildness of the climate, a very relative mildness, certainly, for to Jenghiz Khan the harsh climate of Peking seemed too relaxing, and after each campaign he returned north to spend the summer near Lake Baikal. Similarly, after his victory over Jalal ad-Din, he deliberately shunned India, then at his feet, because, to this man from the Altai, India seemed the very caldron of hell. He was in any case right to mistrust the ease of civilized life, for when his great-grandsons settled into the palaces of Peking and Tabriz, they began at once to degenerate. But as long as the nomad kept the soul of a nomad, he regarded the sedentary man merely as his farmer, and town and tilled land as his farm, both farm and farmer being open to extortion. He roved on horseback along the fringes of ancient empires, exacting regular tribute from those who complied with a relatively good grace or, when the victim was ill-advised enough to refuse payment, plundering open cities in sudden raids. These men were like packs of wolves—and is not the wolf the old Turkic totem?—prowling round herds of deer, to fly at their throats or merely to pick up stragglers and injured beasts. Whirlwind pillage alternating with the exaction of regular tribute—the latter euphemized so far as the Sons of Heaven were concerned by the name of "good-will gift"—was in general a regular feature of the relations between Turko-Mongols and Chinese from the second century B.C. to the seventeenth of this era.

From time to time, however, from among the nomads a man of strong personality would arise, well informed of the ruinous state of the sedentary empires (and these wily barbarians, like the Germanic ones of the fourth century, were wonderfully *au courant* with the Byzantine intrigues of the Chinese imperial court). He would make a pact with one Chinese faction or kingdom against another, or with a banished pretender. He would proclaim himself and his horde confederates of the empire and, under pretext of defending it, move into the border marches. In a generation or two, his grandsons would have acquired enough of the Chinese veneer to take the great step and, all unabashed, ascend the throne of the Sons of Heaven. The exploit of Kublai Khan in the thirteenth century is in this respect merely a repetition of those of Liu Ts'ung and the Toba in the fourth and fifth centuries respectively. In another two or three generations (unless chased over the Great Wall by some national revolt), these Sinicized barbarians, who had acquired nothing from civilization but its softness and its vices without conserving the sternness of the barbarian temperament, became in their turn objects of contempt and their territories the coveted prize of other barbarians who had remained, famished nomads, in the depths of their native steppes. And so the process was repeated. In the fifth century, the Toba arose on the shoulders of the Hsiung-nu and the Hsien-pi to destroy them and take their place. In the twelfth century, to the north of the Khitai, the over-Sinicized Mongols who had been peaceable lords of Peking since the tenth century, there arose the Jurchid; these were Tungus, little more than savages, who within a few months seized the great city, only to submit to Chinese influence in their turn and slumber until, just a century later, they were destroyed by Jenghiz Khan.

The same was as true in the West as in the East. In the Russian steppes of Europe, which are a continuation of those of Asia, there was a similar succession: Attila's Huns were followed by Bulgars (Bolgars), Avars, Hungarians (these were Finno-Ugrians, with a stiffening of Hunnic aristocracy), Khazars, Petchenegs, Cumans, and Jenghiz-Khanites. Similarly, in the lands of Islam, the process of Islamization and Iranization among the Turkish conquerors of Iran and Anatolia forms an exact counterpart to the Sinicizing noted among the Turkic, Mongol, or Tungus conquerors of the Celestial Empire. Here the khan became sultan or padishah, just as there he became a Son of Heaven; and as in China, he had soon to yield to other, rougher khans from the steppes. In Iran a similar sequence of conquest, succession, and destruction can be seen, the Ghaznavid Turks being followed by Seljuk and Khwarizmian Turks, Jenghiz-Khanite Mongols, Timurid Turks, and Shaybanid

Mongols, to say nothing of the Ottoman Turks who, speeding like arrows to the outer rims of the Muslim lands, replaced the dying remnants of the Seljuks in Asia Minor and thence dashed on to their unprecedented triumph, the conquest of Byzantium.

To a higher degree than the Scandinavia of Jordanes, therefore, Continental Asia may be regarded as the matrix of nations, *vagina gentium*, and as the Germania of Asia, destined in its *Völkerwanderungen* to present ancient civilized empires with sultans and Sons of Heaven. These periodic descents by the hordes of the steppe, whose khans ascended the thrones of Changan, Loyang, Kaifeng or Peking, Samarkand, Ispahan or Tabriz (Tauris), Konya or Constantinople, became one of the geographic laws of history. But there was another, opposing law, which brought about the slow absorption of the nomad invaders by ancient civilized lands. This phenomenon was twofold in character. First, there was the demographic aspect. Established as a widely dispersed aristocracy, the barbarian horsemen became submerged in these dense populations, these immemorial anthills. Second, there was the cultural aspect. The civilizations of China and Persia, though conquered, in turn vanquished their wild and savage victors, intoxicating them, lulling them to sleep, and annihilating them. Often, only fifty years after a conquest, life went on as if nothing had happened. The Sinicized or Iranized barbarian, was the first to stand guard over civilization against fresh onslaughts from barbarian lands.

In the fifth century, the Toba lord of Loyang constituted himself the defender of Chinese soil and culture against all Mongols, Hsien-pi, or Juan-juan who aspired to repeat the exploit. In the twelfth century, it was Sanjar the Seljuk who kept his "Watch on the Rhine" on the Oxus and the Jaxartes against all the Oghuz or Kara-Khitai of the Aral or the Ili. The story of Clovis and Charlemagne is repeated on every page of Asiatic history. Just as the Roman civilization in its efforts to resist Saxon and Norman Germanism found reserves of strength in the Frankish energy which it had assimilated, so the civilization of China found its best supporters in these fifth-century Toba, while Arabo-Persian Islam knew no more loyal champion than the valiant Sinjar mentioned above. An even better example is given by those Sinicized or Iranized Turko-Mongols who completed the work of the ancient Kings of Kings or Sons of Heaven. What no Chosroes, no caliph had been able to achieve— possession of the throne of the *basileis* and the ceremonial entrance into Saint Sophia—was accomplished by their unlooked-for successor, the Ottoman padishah of the fifteenth century, amid the acclamation of the Muslim world. In the same way, the dream of Pan-Asiatic dominion cherished by the Han and T'ang was fulfilled by the Yüan emperors of the thirteenth and fourteenth centuries, Kublai Khan and Temür Oljaitu, for the benefit of old China, by making Peking the suzerain capital of Russia, Turkestan, Persia and Asia Minor, Korea, Tibet, and Indochina. Thus the Turko-Mongol conquered the ancient civilizations only to wield his sword in their service. Born to rule, like the Roman of the poet of antiquity, he governed these ancient civilized peoples in keeping with their traditions and their age-long ambitions. From Kublai Khan to K'ang-hsi and Ch'ien-lung, these rulers in their administration of China carried out the program of Chinese imperialism in Asia and, in the Irano-Persian world, brought to fruition the Sassanid and Abbasid thrust toward the golden domes of Constantinople.

Governing races, imperial nations, are few. The Turko-Mongols, like the Romans, are of their number.

Study Questions

1. Why did many civilizations see in the barbarian invasions a form of divine punishment?

2. How were the barbarians "sons of the earth"?

3. What belt of land from Budapest to Manchuria escaped the civilizing process of Europe, Iran, and China? Why?

4. What does Grousset imagine the response of barbarians to sedentary civilization to be?

5. Why were nomads almost always successful in their fights against sedentary civilizations?

6. What finally put an end to the age of pastoral nomadic ascendancy over sedentary civilization?

7. By the time of Christ, what was the general direction of movement of barbarians in the steppe region?

8. What did sedentary historians usually write of the Turko-Mongolian peoples of the steppe?

9. What, by Grousset, is the "paramount fact in human history" related to the barbarians?

10. Why did the Turko-Mongols of the steppes follow their herds?

11. What pattern did a nomad typically follow after taking possession of cultivated land?

12. As long as the nomad "kept the soul of the nomad," how did he regard sedentary civilization?

13. How would nomads occasionally participate in the intrigues of the sedentary civilizations?

14. What often happened to nomads who conquered China?

15. Was this also true of nomads who conquered other sedentary civilizations?

16. Who does Grousset list among the few "governing races, imperial nations" of world history?

B. Khazanov

A. M. Khazanov is one of the most prominent living scholars of the pastoral nomads. Formerly of the Institute of Ethnography at the Academy of Sciences of the U. S. S.R., he immigrated to the United States in the 1980s and now teaches and researches in Wisconsin. Khazanov's formal training is as an anthropologist, but he has the historian's common sense and respectful eye for historical materials and perspectives. His book *Nomads and the Outside World* (Cambridge University Press, 1984) affords important perspectives on the problem of nomadic interaction with the "outside" or non-nomadic world. He concludes that there is no such thing as nomadic "autarky" or complete nomadic isolation from the civilized world; paradoxically, the more purely nomadic a society wishes to remain, the more dependent it is on civilized societies and the commodities that only agricultural civilizations can produce. Khazanov brings important economic perspective on the pastoral nomads and their ecology.

The Phenomenon of Nomadism: Myths and Problems

Poets of different times and of different ages have written many poems (whether or not they are any good is a matter of taste and of the quality of the poems themselves), exalting the beauty of the steppe or, correspondingly, of the desert or the tundra, and the delights of nomadic life. Strictly speaking there is nothing particularly remarkable in this. Indeed, for many traditional societies there is nothing more familiar and therefore already more beautiful than the space surrounding them. But what is far more curious is that in this category of poets there are many non-nomads alongside nomads.

The attitude of sedentaries to nomads has always been ambiguous. The myth of the nomad may be even older than the myth of the 'noble savage'. By the middle of the fifth century B.C. in the writing of the father of history, Herodotus, idealized descriptions of nomad Scythians may be found. Further and even more idealized descriptions may be found in Ephorus. In the fourth century B.C. the Stoics and Cynics seized upon them in order to contrast natural and unspoilt barbarian life with the vices of civilization.

The myth of the nomad even carried over into the Middle Ages. Possibly it played a part in the development of the legend about the eastern kingdom of Prester John, who was called on to free the Christians in the East from the yoke of the infidel.

In modern times both myths (of the savage and of the nomad) have been revitalized, but the myth of the nomad would seem to be the more lasting one. Philosophers have influenced travellers and travellers have influenced scholars. Many sources and ideas have misinformed poets, writers and the general reading public; at the same time there has been a great desire and search for such misinformation about nomadism. In its striking nonconformity with the sedentary life of townsmen, the image of nomadic life has exercised the strong attraction of opposites.

This negative approach to reality has resulted in different outlets, some in the 'realm of fancy'. A stereotyped view of nomads has arisen in which their real or imaginary freedom and political independence almost occupy pride of place. Moreover, despite its poverty and other drawbacks nomadic life thought by nomads themselves and by many onlookers to have one important advantage, which was defined by A.C. Pigou at the beginning of the century as 'quality of life'.

Myths last for as long as there is some need for them. At the same time stereotypes change with difficulty. It could be said that the Hollywood ideal of the cowboy is a direct or indirect descendant of the myth of the nomad. At least they can essentially be seen as one and the same thing.

But myth has a purpose. It is myth which keeps us from knowing the half tones. Apart from its light side the myth of the nomad also has a darker side in which the nomad is perceived almost as the devil incarnate. In China the Confucians simply despised the barbarian nomads, considering them incapable of following a civilized way of life. But in the West, both before and after Jordanes, who believed the Huns were descendants of evil spirits and witches (*Getica*, 121), there were many people who had the same idea. From the times of the biblical prophets the view that nomads are excessively savage and wild has often been associated with the view that they have a particular destiny, as a means through which God can chastise different peoples.

The early Christian authors were familiar with this idea. Not much later Attila was described as no less than the 'scourge of God'. In the Middle Ages similar notions were very widespread and popular; nomads were often included in the register of disasters which listed, amongst others, cholera and the plague.

Once they were no longer associated with disasters, nomads were seen in a more positive, although still exotic light. As it turned out, the dark side of the myth was less lasting than the light. However, this did not mean that the dark side of the myth disappeared altogether. It has been used more than once in colonial and even in post-colonial times by politicians as a means with which to manipulate public opinion. The realm of fancy and the sometimes falsified, or at any rate one-sided, depiction of earthly reality often have turned into neighbours.

The time has come for us to ignore those myths. If nomadism is to be approached as the final result of specialized pastoral economies, and the question posed as to whether nomadism represents more in the evolution and history of mankind than one example of economic adaptation, then we must at once distance ourselves from pressure generated by the self-appraisal of nomads themselves and also from the subjective and emotional evaluations of other, very different societies, in which there are other forms of adaptation and other evolutionary alternatives.

Is it permissible to look on the phenomenon of nomadism as something different from the phenomenon of the sedentary sea-mammal hunters of the Arctic Ocean, or the sedentary fishermen in the deltas of certain rivers on the northwest shores of North America, or even of the different types of shifting horticulturalists in the tropics? Are we not here merely dealing with one level of economic development (a food-producing rather than a food-extracting economy), or with the specificity of the given form of economy (in the final analysis, all forms are specific), or just with something which is quite well known, but not closely connected with academic definitions?

In the final analysis a phenomenon is not only a rare, unusual and unique occurrence, it also may be widespread and, most importantly, global in its consequences. The Tasmanians were a rare phenomenon; the Bushmen of today are still a rare phenomenon. But in my opinion the phenomenon of nomadism also consists in quite the opposite: (a) not only as a specialized occurrence, but also as a very widespread one (particularly in the past), existing all over the world, except in Australia and to a certain degree in America; (b) in its role of linking different societies and cultures; (c) and finally, not only in its economic, but also in its social and historical specificity.

A paradox arises which anticipates the content and conclusions of the book and which may be formulated briefly in the following way: societies based on one of the most specialized types of food-producing economy, in which technology is relatively conservative and has changed little with time, have exercised an essential and, indeed, multifarious influence on the social and political functioning and evolution of non-nomadic societies in which the economy is more diversified and technology more advanced. Amongst nomads themselves pastoral specialization has meant more or less economic one-sidedness and no autarky, and outside the society proper these have led directly to social mobility and heightened political activity.

Most importantly, nomads could never exist on their own without the outside world and its non-nomadic societies, with their different economic systems. Indeed, a nomadic society could only function while the outside world not only existed but also allowed for those reactions from it—reactions which were economic, social, political, cultural, in a word, a multi-faceted response—which ensured that the nomads remained nomads.

In this way, in my view, the important phenomenon of nomadism (while it remains nomadism) really consists in its indissoluble and necessary connection with the outside world; that is to say, with societies which have, different economic and social systems. This book is devoted to the establishing of this thesis.

In the humanities and in anthropology, the reduction of the complex to the simple and of many factors to one often makes more accessible the thought-process of the scholar and the result of his research, but rarely does it truly bear fruit. That which in the natural sciences is possible, or at least considered to be *bon ton*, is not usually applicable to the humanities. In this respect the problem of nomadism serves as a graphic example.

It is not in any respect a closed system. Hence, attempts at defining the operation and evolution of nomadic societies only from the inside, from the viewpoint of ecological or socioeconomic determinism by their own environment, can never be fully successful. Admittedly, such attempts are usually no longer avowed, because the idea of determinism is no longer fashionable; but in practice they are still not infrequently encountered.

The detailed research of many scholars proves that while ecology and economy are certainly amongst the most important factors (although they are not the only ones) which determine the specific character of nomadic societies, these factors still leave a great deal of scope for other variations. Apart from the economic there are also sociopolitical ones. Most importantly, these variations are connected not only with intrinsic factors, but also with extrinsic ones.

The attempts which have been made up to the present day to extend unconditionally the different global and universal systems of the historical development of mankind to include nomads seem unjustifiable. My concern at this point is not to verify or to assess the usefulness of one or other such system; it is a rather different one. Those systems were constructed around data concerning the evolution of sedentary societies (often only in certain defined regions) and mechanically included nomadism, taking no account of the specificity of the latter. However, the connection between nomads and the outside world is one thing; the complete identification of nomads with the outside world is another. To underestimate the idiosyncrasies of nomadic societies is just as dangerous as it is to overestimate them.

The problem of 'nomads and the outside world' is, therefore, so complex and many-sided that there seems to be no way in which it can be simplified. That which is true of one given nomadic society must be reassessed when applied to another nomadic society. Historical perspective must be maintained. That which is true of nomads today may not apply to the nomads of ancient time or of the Middle Ages.

No one scholar could possibly compile something approaching a complete and qualified description of a number, let alone of all nomadic societies; a diachronic analysis, as opposed to a synchronic one, would be even more impossible. That time has passed in which one scholar-compiler may attempt a compendium of the *Weltgeschichte* type.

One way round the problem is to try to find typologies, models and generalizations, i.e. an inevitable and conscious simplification and schematization of reality. If the author is to follow this path he must be prepared for a sceptical reaction from his colleagues; he must realise that there are many superficialities in his research and many very debatable points, possible inaccuracies and even mistakes in his work which, at opportune moments, his colleagues will readily and kindly point out to him. In a word, the author must be prepared not for dithyramhs but for some basic and severe criticism. This author has decided to undertake the task of assessing whether or not there do exist some definite laws about the interrelations between nomads and the outside world (rather than making another study of specific nomadic societies or the nomads of one particular region), for the precise reason that he feels the time has come for such an assessment to be made. It is now as necessary to see the wood in its entirety behind the individual trees as it is to see the individual trees in the wood.

The geographical terminology used in this book may not be familiar to everybody. For reasons which will become clear below the author differentiates between the Near East (Iraq, the Arabian peninsula, the countries of the Fertile Crescent, North Africa down to the Sudan and the Horn of Africa) and the Middle East (Turkey, Iran and Afghanistan). The term Middle East entered common use for rather circumstantial reasons which are connected with the Second World War. As Fisher (1966: 1–2) asserts, 'Up to 1939, there prevailed a somewhat vague and loose division of southern Asia into Near, Middle and Far East . . . The war of 1939 at one stroke removed the question of territorial definition in Western Asia from the academic groves to which it had hitherto been mainly confined. There came the *fait accompli* by which a military province stretching from Iran to Tripolitania was created and named "Middle East".' An anthropologist need scarcely be restricted to such a use.

In accordance with established academic traditions in Russia and partly in continental Europe, in this book Middle Asia is differentiated from Inner (Central) Asia; in the Anglo-Saxon tradition both regions are referred to under the general term, Central Asia. Historically the regions are very closely connected. However, anyone who has visited them or who is acquainted with literature about the geography of the area knows that there are important environmental differences between them. Consequently, for this author Middle Asia comprises the region which is flanked in the north by the Aral Sea and the Kazakh steppes, in the south by the Kopet-Dagh and Hindu-Kush, in the west by the Capian Sea, and in the east by the Pamirs. Inner Asia is that region which comprises Kashgaria, Jungaria, Mongolia and Tibet, and is flanked in the south by the Himalayas and in the northeast by the peaks of the Inshan and Great Khingan.

In this book more space is devoted to materials about the nomads of the Eurasian steppes, semi-deserts and deserts than to materials about nomads of other regions. This is for no other particular reason than that it just so happens that most of the work about nomads and nomadism which the author has published in the past has centered on this region. Both from his reading of relevant literature and his fieldwork—ethnographical in Middle Asia, Kalmuckia and Daghestan, and archaeological in the South Russian steppes, Middle Asia and the North Caucasus—he knows Eurasian nomads and nomadism more thoroughly than he does the nomads of any other region.

An entire chapter of this book is devoted to the origins of pastoral nomadism. This is not only because the author is not satisfied with the current hypotheses and theories. He also considers that in a book about the interrelations between nomads and the sedentary world it would seem to be both interesting and expedient to begin the history of the interrelations *ab ovo*. I cannot but agree with Boas (1940:305): 'To understand a phenomenon we have not only to know what it is, but also how it came into being.'

It is partly for this reason that particular attention is paid wherever possible in this book to nomads of ancient times and of the Middle Ages, and partly also for reasons of a different kind. The nomads of today directly or indirectly already have been drawn into contemporary economic and political systems of the sedentary world. However, as a rule, this has happened by different means and on a different basis from the way it did in the past. The character of the interrelations between nomads and the outside world has undergone qualitative changes. Changes now occur in nomadic societies so quickly that anthropologists often do not have time to record them. Thus, where the present century is referred to in this book the use of the present tense is often purely conditional.

Of course the modern period did not begin everywhere at the same time. But the origin of the process which fundamentally changed the position of nomads in the world was already determined in the late Middle Ages by the emergence of strong centralized states, such as the Ottoman, Russian and Ch'ing empires. The colonial period enabled this process to intensify and become more widespread; and in post-colonial times corresponding tendencies only increased and became more firmly established. The question as to whether nomadism can survive in the contemporary world raises serious doubts. Opportunities for nomadism to adapt itself to the outside world are few and far between. Once again Cain is killing Abel, slowly but surely and with very little standing in the way, this time insisting on the most noble of intentions. It is true that today, by way of exception, the short-lived revival of nomadism in certain areas may be observed. But the revival is local in character and scarcely will last for long. Consequently, in many instances it is risky to extrapolate about the past from contemporary field work and its conclusions without duly considering the changes in the character of the interrelations between nomads and the outside world and their consequences, which have taken place over the course of the last two or three hundred years.

But the data about the nomads of ancient times and the Middle Ages have one essential defect. As a whole facts are relatively few and far between and, moreover, they were collected not by professional anthropologists, but by people who at best were well acquainted with nomads and their way of life but who, on the other hand, had not read Lattimore, Barth or Dyson-Hudson. Nevertheless, any attempt to trace the particularities of nomadism not only in its present rather sad state, but also in a historical context, must take these facts into consideration.

The position is made somewhat easier when reference is to the ecological and productive fundamentals of nomadism, which are least well documented in the historical sources but which, on the other hand, have changed relatively little with the passing of time; in this sphere extrapolation from contemporary facts or facts from the not too distant past is not only inevitable, but even permissible within certain limits, although many reservations must also be acknowledged. But when reference is to the sociopolitical organization of nomads and, particularly, to concrete forms of their interrelations with sedentary peoples, reference to historical sources is imperative. Fortunately, since ancient times the sedentary world has not only been concerned with mythopoesis when dealing with nomads.

Discoveries are not made in the course of general observation, but at the time when it becomes the common interest of mankind for them to be made. Nomads, it would appear, have never taken any initiative on this account. Their knowledge of the outside world has remained for the most part utilitarian. On the other hand, from the time of its first acquaintance with nomads the outside world has been interested in different aspects of the lives of nomads and this interest, at first utilitarian and emotional, gradually became more academic.

The detailed research of that theme is the subject of another book, which should be very useful and interesting, but it has yet to be written. Here I shall only briefly mention the basic stages in the development of the study of nomads which is far from complete, if indeed there is anything which is complete in this world.

Even before the emergence of real nomadism the ancient states of Western Asia were forced to have dealings with mobile pastoralists and semi-nomads. Descriptions of their way of life stress how unusual they seemed to sedentaries, but there is no special ethnographical information in these descriptions.

In the first centuries of the last thousand years B.C. the pastoralists and semi-nomads of the previous thousand years B.C. began to be replaced in certain cultural areas of Western Asia by real nomads who often were migrants from other areas. Those were times of shock and terror, caused by the unwelcome appearance of a menacing and hitherto unknown force. The biblical prophets give what is perhaps the best description of all this (see, for example, Jeremiah 5.15–17). In the Bible and in Assyro-Babylonian sources some facts are to be found about the political history of nomads in this period, but there is no purely ethnographical information.

The first stage in the study of nomadism comprises antiquity and part of the Middle Ages in which the ancient tradition was continued and preserved. In this period nomads become a constant, although usually a disturbing and often disagreeable factor in world order. Administrators and military commanders in sedentary lands who had to have dealings with nomads rarely bothered with academic research. Scholars for the most part lived far removed from nomads and, with only individual exceptions, were usually content with standard descriptions of the way of life and mores of nomads, which were so different from the way of life and mores of agriculturalists and townsmen. These descriptions report the absence of agriculture, movements with livestock according to availability of grass and water, and the absence of fixed movement patterns; they are repeated sometimes almost word for word in Greek, Roman, Chinese and even in some medieval sources, and often appear to be verbatim copies of each other (see Herodotus IV.46 on the Scythians, or Diodorus IX.94.2 on the Nabataeans, or Ssu-Ma Ch'ien [Syma Tsian], *Shih Chi*, Ch. 110 on the Hsiung-nu, or Ammianus Marcellinus XIV.4.3.5 on the Saracens and XXXI.2.10 on the Huns).

Nevertheless, the ancient tradition provides us with an idea of a particular nomadic world within which all the individual peoples are similar, but at the same time quite dissimilar from other peoples living outside the confines of that particular world. This idea, reinforced by concrete empirical experience as well as by speculation, has turned out to be very long-lasting. Scholars in the Caliphate succeeded in widely disseminating the ideas of their predecessors in antiquity. According to the twelfth-century author Marvazi who, with reference to Hippocrates (now identified as Pseudo-Hippocrates), wrote about the nomads of the east-European steppes, the Scythians of the distant past had become the Turkic peoples of his day; at least in no essential way were the two peoples different, for the same author goes on to insist that '. . . in Europe all the Turkic peoples are alike, but they are like no other people'.

For the Greeks in antiquity the word 'Scythian' was associated with a specific ethnicity and generally with the nomads of the North; the word 'Turkic' meant much the same for scholars in the Caliphate. Such views were reinforced by ideas about the nomads' particular type of economy and its dependence on natural environment. The beginnings of the ecological trend in the study of nomads are thus to be found in antiquity.

At the same time it was during this early stage that the first isolated attempts to include nomads in the general schemata of the development of mankind were made; true, these mythologized about a lost golden age or the antithesis of this, or else they can be found in rather more scholarly form in the tripartite theory worked out by Varro. Finally, the wisest and most far-sighted of the more pragmatic politicians, whose aims in examining the social and political peculiarities of nomads were eminently practical, concluded that in these peculiarities were contained both the strength and weakness of nomadism. Maybe because of pragmatic necessity, therefore, this stage witnesses the beginnings of the sociopolitical trend in the study of nomads.

The second stage begins in the Middle Ages and includes part of the modern period. Partly it continues the traditions of the preceding period, extending and enriching them, partly it witnesses much which was new in the study of nomads, preparing the way for the following period.

Of course the emotions and impressions of many of those who personally lived through or witnessed the invasions of nomads scarcely differ from the feelings of the biblical prophets as they describe the descent of the Cimerians and Scythians on Western Asia.

But Rashid al-Din and Ibn Khaldun were not ruled by their emotions. As politicians they recognized that nomads were an immutable part of political life. They were also scholars. Thus, they are worthy of special credit. In their works the connection between nomadism and a specific natural environment is for the first time given serious consideration: they make considerable progress in the study of the social organization of nomads. Rashid al-Din was one of the first to pay serious attention to the meaning of kinship and genealogical ties for nomads. And finally, it is in the works of both these scholars (and also of their less well-known precursors and followers) that nomads for the first time become not a by-product or antipode of civilization, an abortive line of history, but an integral, constituent and even vital part of history. The whole cyclical conception of civilization devised by Ibn Khaldun would have been impossible without nomads.

The third stage in the study of nomads is connected with the establishing of modern history and anthropology. In Western Europe the horrors of nomad invasions were increasingly becoming something of the past, and so the study of nomadism here became less empirical than it was in the East. In the West attempts were renewed, or rather they began afresh, to define in general terms the place of nomads and pastoralists in evolution and history.

The tripartite theory was extremely popular in the eighteenth and nineteenth centuries; but in the minds of many scholars it left open many of the same questions which had troubled Ibn Khaldun. Many of those scholars tried not only to define, but also to evaluate the role of nomads in the general development of mankind, and in the origins of the state and of civilization. At the same period as Montesquieu and certain other scholars were trying to establish the egalitarian character of nomadic societies, Fergusson and Adam Smith were claiming that the development of pastoralism led to social differentiation. Kant saw the origins of statehood in the conflict between nomads and agriculturalists. Hegel, on the other hand, linked nomads with the second prehistoric period which preceded the emergence of the state, even though it is characterized by conflicts.

In this way, towards the beginning of the nineteenth century, a specific tendency was formulated, or perhaps it would be better described as a state of inertia in the theoretical study of nomads; nomads and pastoralists (no precise differentiation was made between the two) were looked upon not so much as a particular ethnographical phenomenon, but as a factor in the general development of mankind. Nomads were being characterized not only by sedentaries, but by sedentaries who were civilized townsmen. Nomads were basically of interest to scholars in so far as they could be fitted into different historical conceptions and schemata, which were based on the agricultural and urban development of society and crowned by civilizations created by agriculturalists and townsmen.

It is true that in the eighteenth century, and particularly in the nineteenth, yet another side of the study of nomads, which for a long time had had only a tenuous connection with the one mentioned above, rapidly began to emerge. Philosophers and historians remained indoors, confined to their studies, to argue about nomadism, but field researchers were out at work in Africa, the Near and Middle East, the Eurasian steppes and Inner Asia. These researchers were not, however, professional anthropologists and were often moved by purely practical necessities, but they were responsible for the first specific descriptions of specific nomadic peoples. These descriptions were often not very skilled, even less were they specialized, but what they did was to provide a quantity of much needed primary material which was ready for reworking.

The fourth stage in the study of nomads can be dated to the first half of the twentieth century. Characteristic of this stage, rather surprisingly, was the fact that, on the one hand, the study of nomadism became much more anthropological and, on the other hand, a distinct gap formed between the development of anthropological theory and its application to nomadic societies, despite the fact that field research had begun to be undertaken by professionals. This state of affairs is noted by N. Dyson-Hudson (1972) who offers an explanation for it.

Admittedly, in general theories of the *Kulturkreislehre* type, materials relating to nomads are allotted a great deal of space, but they are only used as examples which corroborate theoretical positions already formulated. Admittedly, such scholars of the end of the last century and the beginning of the present one as Ratzel, Gumplowicz, Oppenheimer and Thurnwald showed a theoretical interest in nomads, but only as an active factor in the 'conquest theory' of the origin of the state which they were developing at the time; with this theory they were carrying on the old line of research about nomads.

At the same time, however, there were new theories and new theoretical approaches: a real, socio-cultural and environmental adaptation, functional-structural, cross-cultural, psychological, neo-evolutionistic and ecological. They were many and varied, but made comparatively little use of data about nomads, and in turn did not have any great influence on the research into nomadic societies.

The gap between historical and anthropological research in the field of nomadism has not narrowed, rather it would seem to have become even more pronounced. In the many concepts of the evolution and history of mankind which have been put forward by different scholars, adhering to different schools of thought, with the exception of Toynbee's works, nowhere are nomads apportioned a fitting, let alone, a special place. At the same time anthropologists have concentrated on synchronic research and rarely resorted to using historical materials. In every respect Lattimore's brilliant book (1940) stands out on its own.

In the Soviet Union the study of nomadism has been carried out within the framework of the Marxist line of scientific thought as formulated in the thirties and forties. Characteristic of this period are the predominance of speculative calculations over concrete research, of theoretical office-work over fieldwork, and the desire to prove that the development of nomadic societies is in no essential way different from the development of sedentary societies, for both correspond to historical materialism's accepted postulates about the universal socioeconomic stages which consistently succeed each other. It is hardly surprising that it was in this period that the slave-owning and feudal stages among nomads were 'discovered'. On the other hand, because the Soviet scholars working in those years were under the indubitable influence of Marxism and also because their academic tradition was different to the one which existed in the West, there was no discrepancy between historical, archaeological and anthropological theories in their research.

The fifth stage in the study of nomadism begins in the West and in the Soviet Union at roughly the same period (somewhere in the mid fifties) and continues up to the present day. However, it is possible that a new stage began in the mid seventies. Whether or not this is the case only the future will tell.

Characteristic of this fifth stage is a marked expansion of field research into nomads and an increase in the number of scholars working on different problems connected with nomads and nomadism. Materials about nomads have caused many different spheres of contemporary anthropological thought to begin to be adapted and scrutinized thoroughly. In the Soviet Union political changes in the post-Stalin period have been reflected in the academic world; thus in Soviet anthropology a great deal more attention has begun to be paid to the ways in which nomadic societies differ from sedentary ones, to the particularities of their sociopolitical organization and to the specific ways in which they function and develop. Discussion of these problems began in the fifties and continues in a diverse form up to the present day. In recent years the ecological approach to the study of nomads to some degree has been extended.

When referring to the particularities of the fifth stage I have deliberately avoided mentioning the names of scholars who are connected with specific theoretical approaches and paradigms. It is extremely difficult when referring to colleagues who are still alive, still working actively and fruitfully, to avoid subjective evaluations. Consequently, it is best that the description of their theoretical views either be left to them themselves, or to historiographers of the future.

I have also deliberately chosen to avoid at this point a discussion of the comparative merits and shortcomings of specific works about nomads which have been published recently. I am not doing this out of tact or fear of offending one or other of my colleagues. . . . But to criticize is easier than it is to create. Thus, I should like to stress . . . that it is my strong conviction that all the scholarly works which I have read about nomadism, old and new alike, are both valuable and useful, and that all academic approaches in research into the phenomenon of nomadism have their advantages. This in no way entails wholehearted agreement with them; freedom from prejudice is all that is required.

At the same time, however, I should like to stress yet another factor. Now that a sizeable amount of material has been accumulated and theoretical research has made significant progress, nomadism once again must be studied in all its complexity, not only in its static but also in its dynamic functioning. It must be studied as an aggregate whole with its inner and outer systems, structures, functions and ties, not only as an isolated variant of local, specific or multilineal evolution, but also as an essential and integral factor in human history.

Finally, it is necessary to put an end to the almost complete predominance of synchronic research and to return to diachrony its proper place in the anthropology of nomadism. With reference to nomads I can only repeat the incisive conclusion of Evans-Pritchard, reached in the fifties: '. . . by and by anthropology will have the choice between being history and being nothing'. Of course, work with historical sources (as, incidentally, with any others) is linked with specific difficulties; of course, these sources are not complete, at times they are imprecise. Nevertheless, much useful and indispensable anthropological information can be extracted from them. A paleontologist will not turn up his nose at a tiny piece of bone, in the same way as an archaeologist will not do so at the handle of a broken pot; they are satisfied with what they can find. In order to become a palaeoanthropologist, an anthropologist must reconcile himself to the fact that he must make do with available historical material and learn to use it in the best possible way. In comparison to historical criticism, anthropological criticism of written sources is as yet in a state of infancy. However, in my view, the latter contains reasonable possibilities and perspectives.

The belittling of reports made by early travellers and observers of nomadism is quite unjustified. Of course, it is a pity that neither Volney or Burckhardt read Emmanuel Marx or Bonte, although there are still advantages in this fact. But does this mean that their reports are then of no value to the anthropologist? Considering the changes in nomadic societies which have occurred since the times when their accounts were published, anthropologists are faced with two alternatives: either they can confine themselves to a study of the situation in the present day; or else they can use the materials of their precursors and, fully aware of contemporary scientific knowledge and methods, they can try to extract the maximum amount of useful information from these materials, rather than just point to their obvious inadequacies.

The union, or at least the dialogue, between anthropology and history is perfectly practicable and it promises reasonable fruit. There are precedents for this already, for example, in classical studies. In order to avoid digression here it will be sufficient to list such English scholars of past generations as Andrew Lang, Jane Harrison, Gilbert Murray, H.M. Chadwick and, moreover, our contemporary, M.I. Finley. If history up to now has gained more from this union than anthropology, this is only because historians began to use anthropological materials and anthropological methods of research before anthropologists began to use historical ones. Finley (1975:108) is correct when he writes, '. . . beginning with Malinowski, anthropologists over-reacted to the historical conjecturing and the unilinear evolutionism of their predecessors by rejecting not only their bad methods but the subject of their inquiry as well, a procedure which, though understandable, is not justifiable'. I can only add to this that the not uncommon identification of Marxism or unilinear evolutionism with historical explanation in anthropology is scarcely justified. The historical approach is entirely compatible with the different anthropological schools and paradigms.

The phenomenon of nomadism once again needs to be looked at as a whole, with both the research of the past and contemporary academic conceptions being taken into account. The ideal situation would be to see once again the whole wood in its entirety, without at the same time letting any one tree out of sight. This task is too much for one scholar, but this author is glad that he is not alone in his aspirations. Efforts in this direction are now being made and, it is to be hoped, they will continue to be made in the future. Surely, in the end, *de nihilo nihil*.

Nomadism as a Distinct Form of Food-Producing Economy

What is nomadism?

Terminology is something about which we should agree, not argue. Unfortunately, and in this respect nomads are no exception, this rule is often not observed in practice. The term 'nomads' means different things to different scholars; however, for a long time now it has been used to describe two basic tendencies. On the one hand, some scholars have defined nomads as all those leading a mobile way of life independent of its economic specificity; other scholars have described nomads as extensive and mobile pastoralists who either have nothing at all to do with agriculture, or who are occupied with agriculture to a limited degree in the capacity of a secondary and supplementary activity.

The first notion of nomadism, which had gained too wide a currency appears gradually to be going out of use; however, it may still be encountered (e.g., de Planhol, 1966:277 calls the Australian Aborigines nomads; Lee and De Vore, 1968:11–12 call all hunters and gatherers in general nomads; while Averkieva, 1970:3f., uses the term for mounted hunters of bison; see also Murdock and Wilson, 1972:256–7; Simonsen, 1972: 190).

In my view, wandering hunters and gatherers, on the one hand, and mobile pastoralists, on the other, have too little in common to unite them under a single label. The bases of their economy, food-extracting in the first instance, food-producing in the second, are different in principle; thus their reasons for being mobile are different and the character of the mobility is different. Kroeber (1947) obviously had this in mind when he contrasted 'pastoral nomadic' with 'primitive nomadic'. In the same way, the term 'nomads' is not applicable to other mobile groups, whether ethnic-professional groups such as gypsies, or the so-called 'maritime nomads' of Southeast Asia, or shifting horticulturalists, or certain groups of workers in contemporary industrial societies (so-called industrial mobility).

Consequently, hunters and gatherers who do not lead a sedentary way of life are best described by the term 'wandering' (correspondingly, semi-wandering, semi-sedentary, etc.), and mobile extensive pastoralists by the term 'nomadic'. Recently a similar view has been held by many scholars (see, for e.g., Forde, 1963:33–4, 406; von Wissman and von Kussmaul, 1959:874; Krader, 1966:408–9; Spooner, 1973:3; Khazanov, 1975:5–6; Andrianov, 1978:120). In this way we are returning to the original meaning of the term and the sense which the ancient Greeks attributed to the words 'νομάζ, νομάδες, νομαδιχός. 'And the wind returneth again according to his circuits [Eccl. 1.6].'

However, if all mobile pastoralists are described as nomads this once again leads to an excessively broad and imprecise use of the term, because there are very many different forms of mobile pastoralism. It is obvious that the definition of pastoral nomadism as a particular form of food-producing economy should be based on the sum total of those economic particularities in which it differs from other kinds, forms and even varieties of economic activity.

In my view, the most important characteristics defining the economic essence of pastoral nomadism are: (1) Pastoralism is the predominant form of economic activity. (2) Its extensive character connected with the maintenance of herds all year round on a system of free-range grazing without stables. (3) Periodic[1] mobility in accordance with the demands of pastoral economy within the boundaries of specific grazing territories, or between these territories (as opposed to migrations). (4) The participation in pastoral mobility of all or the majority of the population (as opposed, for example, to the management of herds on distant pastures by specialist herdsmen, into which only a minority is involved in pastoral migrations). (5) The orientation of production towards the requirements of subsistence (as opposed to the capitalist ranch or dairy farming of today). This fifth characteristic today no longer applies, or applies only in part to certain groups of pastoral nomads which have been drawn into the world market system; but it was fairly characteristic of pastoral nomadism in the past, although even then pastoral nomadism was not economically self-sufficient. Production was not at that time aimed at specific profits, although often it was directed to quite a considerable extent towards exchange.

These are the basic economic characteristics of nomadism. On the one hand, they underline its specificity as a distinct form of food-producing economy, thereby distinguishing nomadism from other kinds and forms of economic activity and indicating its limitations; on the other hand, they permit us to unite under one heading and systematize similar types and sub-types of economic activity (in the given instance of pastoral nomadism), over and above other secondary characteristics in which they may differ. Finally, with those characteristics, to a greater or lesser extent, are connected the basic economic, social, political and cultural parameters of nomadism, and even its interrelations with the outside world.

In this way pastoral nomadism may be defined from the economic point of view as a distinct form of food-producing economy in which extensive mobile pastoralism is the predominant activity, and in which the majority of the population is drawn into periodic pastoral migrations. Perhaps one can also add that pastoral nomadism, in common with the other main forms of economy, is associated with a particular level in the development of technology. This level characterizes the period between two revolutions (including their consequences): the Neolithic and the Industrial.

According to the suggested definition, pastoral nomadism is a single form of food-producing economy which remains different from other food-extracting economies (for example, from different forms of hunting, fishing and gathering), and also from other food-producing economies (for example, from different forms of slash and burn and shifting horticulture, plough agriculture, etc.). However, it must also be admitted that pastoral nomadism is not completely separate economically from other food-producing economies, rather it is linked with them by a series of transitional forms at the basis of which lies the gradually diminishing specific position of pastoralism. The appropriate boundary-line is not always drawn between these forms (see, for example, Kroeber, 1947:323–4; Markov, 1976:209; Marx, 1977:344–5) and this sometimes leads to a distorted picture of nomadism. Thus the terms 'pastoral' and 'pastoralism', although they are very widely used, in themselves are too imprecise and unspecific.

Study Questions

1. What, according to Khazanov, is the "myth of the nomad"?
2. How did some Biblical prophets view the nomads?
3. Can nomadism exist independent of the outside, non-nomadic world?
4. What region of pastoralism does Khazanov pay the most attention to?
5. Khazanov makes this intriguing statement about the chances for nomadism to survive in the modern world: "Once again Cain is killing Abel. " What might he mean by this? Look up the story of Cain and Abel in the Scriptures. What was Cain's offering? Abel's?
6. Khazanov says that during the first centuries of the last thousand years B.C., pastoralists and semi-nomads began to be replaced by "real nomads," whose presence was noted by Biblical prophets. Look up Jeremiah 5:15–17. How are the nomads described in this passage?
7. What is common to Greek, Roman, and Chinese descriptions of the way of life of the nomads?
8. What did the German philosopher Immanuel Kant (1724–1804) see in the conflict between nomads and agriculturalists?
9. What characterized the "fourth stage" of the study of the nomads during the first half of the twentieth century?
10. What, according to the anthropologist Evans-Pritchard, will anthropology soon ("by and by") have the choice of being?
11. What is Khazanov's opinion of the reports on nomads made by earlier (historical) travellers and observers?
12. Why, according to Khazanov, do wandering hunter-gatherers on the one hand and mobile pastoralists on the other have too little in common to label them both as "nomadic"?
13. What, according to Khazanov, is the best label to use in describing hunter-gatherers?
14. What five characteristics are the basis of pastoral nomadism?
15. According to Khazanov, is pastoral nomadism a "food-extracting" or a "food-producing" economy? Why?

---

1. It is necessary to differentiate between regular pastoral migrations (for example the mobility of the nomads of the Eurasian steppes to seasonal pastures) and irregular ones (for example amongst the nomads of the Sahara); but in pastoral nomadism sooner or later mobility is inevitable.

II.

The Scythians

The Scythians were pastoral nomadic horsemen who inhabited the steppe region north of the Black Sea and flourished from the eighth through second centuries B.C. They were among the earliest true pastoral nomads known to man. Classical Greek authors were fascinated with the Scythians, seeing in them an attractive primitive simplicity they thought somehow absent in the civilized world they knew.

Herodotus takes up the Scythians with obvious interest, even fascination. His account of them is one of the main sources on the Scythians available to historians.

A. Herodotus

The Greek historian Herodotus (c. 485–425 B.C.) was born in a Greek colony on the coast of Asia Minor. After his colony was liberated from the Persians during the Persian Wars (499–479 B.C.), Herodotus travelled widely in the Mediterranean world gathering historical, mythological, ethnographical, and geographical material for a history of the wars and their causes. Herodotus was genuinely interested in the "barbarians" or non-Greek peoples of the ancient world, and in investigating the causes of the Persian Wars he was clearly fascinated with much of the captivating anecdotal nature of the historical memory and traditions of the barbarians he encountered.

The Roman orator Cicero (106–43 B.C.) called Herodotus the "father of history," but Herodotus was not always careful to investigate or collaborate the claims or traditions of his informants; sometimes it seems that for him, an engaging and entertaining historical narrative was more important or desirable than strict accuracy of historical detail. Herodotus made the material he gathered the subject of captivating lectures or stories he delivered to enthusiastic and attentive crowds.

Herodotus's history survives virtually intact. Book Four of his History covers the attempts of the Persian ruler Darius (548–486 B.C.) to defeat the Scythians. His eye for (and interest in) the details of the non-Greeks' ways of life is apparent in his passages on the Scythians, in which he describes their religion, customs, and ways in warfare. He might have admired the Scythians for the simplicity of their way of life and their ultimate ability to frustrate, as did the Greeks, the ultimate military designs and ambitions of the Persians.

Herodotus
The Histories

Translated by Aubrey de Sélincourt

Having described the natural resources of the country, I will go on to give some account of the people's customs and beliefs. The only gods the Scythians worship are Hestia (their chief deity), Zeus, and Earth (whom they believe to be the wife of Zeus), and, as deities of secondary importance, Apollo, Celestial, Aphrodite, Heracles, and Ares. These are recognized by the entire nation; the Royal Scythians also offer sacrifice to Poseidon. In the Scythian language Hestia is *Tabiti*, Zeus (very properly, in my opinion) *Papaeus*, Earth *Api*, Apollo *Oetosyrus*, Aphrodite *Argimpasa*, Poseidon *Thagimasadas*.

It is not there custom to make statues, or to build altars and temples, in honour of any god except Ares. The method of sacrifice is everywhere and in every case the same: the victim has its front feet tied together, and the person who is performing the ceremony gives a pull on the rope from behind and throws the animal down, calling, as he does so, upon the name of the appropriate god; then he slips a noose round the victim's neck, pushes a short stick under the cord and twists it until the creature is choked. No fire is lighted; there is no offering of first-fruits, and no libation. As soon as the animal is strangled, he is skinned, and then comes the boiling of the flesh. This has called for a little inventiveness, because there is no wood in Scythia to make a fire with; the method the natives adopt after skinning the animal is to strip the flesh from the bones and put it into a cauldron—if, that is, they happen to possess one: these cauldrons are made in the country, and resemble Lesbian mixing-bowls in shape, though they are much larger—and then make a fire of the bones underneath it. In the absence of a cauldron, they put all the flesh into the animal's paunch, mix water with it, and boil it like that over the bone-fire. The bones burn very well, and the paunch easily contains all the meat once it has been stripped off. In this way an ox, or any other sacrificial beast, is ingeniously made to boil itself. When the meat is cooked, the sacrificer offers a portion of both flesh and entrails by throwing it on the ground in front of him. All sorts of cattle are offered in sacrifice, but most commonly horses.

Ceremonies in honour of Ares are conducted differently. In every district, at the seat of government. Ares has his temple; it is of a peculiar kind, and consists of an immense heap of brushwood, three furlongs each way and somewhat less in height. On top the heap is levelled off square, like a platform, accessible on one side but rising sheer on the other three. Every year a hundred and fifty waggon-loads of sticks are added to the pile, to make up for the constant settling caused by rains, and on the top of it is planted an ancient iron sword, which serves for the image of Ares. Annual sacrifices of horses and other cattle are made to this sword, which, indeed, claims a greater number of victims than any other of their gods. Prisoners of war are also sacrificed to Ares, but in their case the ceremony is different from that which is used in the sacrifice of animals: one man is chosen out of a every hundred; wine is poured on his head, and his throat cut over a bowl; the bowl is then carried to the platform on top of the wood-pile, and the blood in it poured out over the sword. While this goes on above, another ceremony is being enacted below, close against the pile: this consists in cutting off. The right hands and arms of the prisoners who have been slaughtered, and tossing them into the air. This done, and the rest of the ceremony over, the worshippers go away. The victims' arms and hands are left to lie where they fall, separate from the trunks. They never use pigs for sacrifice and will not even breed them anywhere in the country.

As regards war, the Scythian custom is for every man to drink the blood of the first man he kills. The heads of all enemies killed in battle are taken to the king; if he brings a head, a soldier is admitted to his share of the loot; no head, no loot. He strips the skin off the head by making a circular cut round the ears and shaking out the skull; he then scrapes the flesh off the skin with the rib of an ox, and when it is clean works it in his fingers until it is supple, and fit to be used as a sort of handkerchief. He hangs these handkerchiefs on the bridle of his horse, and is very proud of them. The finest fellow is the man who has the greatest number. Many Scythians sew a number of scalps together and make cloaks out of them, like the ones peasants wear, and often, too, they take the skin, nails and all, off the right hands and arms of dead enemies and use it to cover their quivers with—having discovered the fact that human skin is not only tough, but white, as white as almost any skin. Sometimes they flay a whole body, and stretch the skin on a wooden frame which they carry around with them when they ride. They have a special way of dealing with the actual skulls—not with all of them, but only those of their worst enemies: they saw off the part below the eyebrows, and after cleaning out what remains stretch a piece of rawhide round it on the outside. If a man is poor, he is content with that, but a rich man goes farther and gilds the inside of the skull as well. In either case the skull is then used to drink from. They treat the skulls of their kinsmen in the same way, in cases where quarrels have occurred and a man has been beaten in fight in the presence of the king. When important visitors arrive, these skulls are passed round and the host tells the story of them: how they were once his relatives and made war against him, and how he defeated them—all of which passes for a proof of courage. Once a year the governor of each district mixes a bowl of wine, from which every Scythian who has killed his man in battle has the right to drink. Those who have no dead enemy to their credit are not allowed to touch the wine, but have to sit by themselves in disgrace—the worst, indeed, which they can suffer. Any man, on the contrary, who has killed a great many enemies, has two cups and drinks from both of them at once.

There are many soothsayers in Scythia, and their method is to work with willow rods. They bring great bundles of them, which they put down on the ground; then they untie them, lay out each rod separately, and pronounce their prophecy. While they are speaking it, they collect the rods into a bundle again as before. This is the native mode of divination in Scythia; but the class of effeminate persons called 'Enarees' use a different method, which they say was taught them by Aphrodite: these people take a piece of the inner bark of the lime-tree and cut it into three pieces, which they keep twisting and untwisting round their fingers as they prophesy.

When the king of Scythia falls sick, he sends for three of the most reputable soothsayers, who proceed to practise their arts, in the way I have described; more often than not they declare that such and such a person (whose name they mention) has sworn falsely by the king's hearth—it being customary in Scythia to use this form of oath for the most solemn purposes. The supposed culprit is at once arrested and brought into the king's presence, where he is charged by the soothsayers, who tell him that their powers of divination have revealed that he has sworn by the king's hearth and perjured himself and that his perjury is the cause of the king's sickness. The man, of course, denies the charge, and makes a great fuss, whereupon the king sends for more soothsayers—six this time instead of three—who also bring their skill to bear. Should they convict the accused of perjury, he is beheaded without more ado, and his property is divided by lot amongst the first three soothsayers; if, however, the new six acquit him, more are brought in, and, if need be, still more again, and if, in the final result, the majority declare for the man's innocence, the law is that the three original ones should be executed. The method of execution is this: a cart is filled with sticks and harnessed to oxen; the guilty men, gagged and bound hand and foot, are thrust down amongst the sticks, which are then set alight, and the oxen scared off at a run. Often the oxen are burnt to death together with the soothsayers; often, too, the pole of the cart is burnt through soon enough to allow them to escape with a scorching. Peccant soothsayers—'lying prophets' as they are called—are burnt to death in this way for other crimes besides the one I have described. When the king orders an execution, he does not allow the criminal's sons to survive him: all males are put to death, but not the females, who are in no way harmed.

When Scythians swear an oath or make a solemn compact, they fill a large earthenware bowl with wine and drop into it a little of the blood of the two parties to the oath, having drawn it either by a prick with a awl or a slight cut with a knife; then they dip into the bowl a sword, some arrows, a battle-axe, and a javelin, and speak a number of prayers; lastly, the two contracting parties and their chief followers drink the mixture of wine and blood.

The burial-place of the Scythian kings is in the country of the Gerrhi, near the spot where the Borysthenes first becomes navigable. When a king dies, they dig a great square pit, and, when it is ready, they take up the corpse, which has been previously prepared in the following way: the belly is slit open, cleaned out, and filled with various aromatic substances, crushed galingale, parsley-seed, and anise; it is then sewn up again and the whole body coated over with wax. In this condition it is carried in a waggon to a neighbouring tribe within the Scythian dominions, and then on to another, taking the various tribes in turn; and in the course of its progress, the people who successively receive it, follow the custom of the Royal Scythians and cut a piece from their ears, shave their hair, make circular incisions on their arms, gash their foreheads and noses, and thrust arrows through their left hands. On each stage of the journey those who have already been visited join the procession, until at last the funeral cortège, after passing through every part of the Scychian dominions, finds itself at the place of burial amongst the Gerrhi, the most northerly and remote of Scythian tribes. Here the corpse is laid in the tomb on a mattress, with spears fixed in the ground on either side to support a roof of withies laid on wooden poles, while in other parts of the great square pit various members of the king's household are buried beside him: one of his concubines, his butler, his cook, his groom, his steward, and his chamberlain—all of them strangled. Horses are buried too, and gold cups (the Scythians do not use silver or bronze), and a selection of his other treasures. This ceremony over, everybody with great enthusiasm sets about raising a mound of earth, each competing with his neighbour to make it as big as possible. At the end of a year another ceremony takes place: they take fifty of the best of the king's remaining servants, strangle and gut them, stuff the bodies with chaff, and sew them up again—these servants are native Scythians, for the king has no bought slaves, but chooses people to serve him from amongst his subjects. Fifty of the finest horses are then subjected to the same treatment. The next step is to cut a number of wheels in half and to fix them in pairs, rim-downwards, to stakes driven into the ground, two stakes to each half-wheel; then stout poles are driven lengthwise through the horses from tail to neck, and by means of these the horses are mounted on the wheels, in such a way that the front pairs support the shoulders and the rear pairs the belly between the thighs. All four legs are left dangling clear of the ground. Each horse is bitted and bridled, the bridle being led forward and pegged down. The bodies of the men are dealt with in a similar way: straight poles are driven up through the neck, parallel with the spine, and the lower protruding ends fitted into sockets in the stakes which run through the horses; thus each horse is provided with one of the young servants to ride him. When horses and riders are all in place around the tomb, they are left there, and the mourners go away. When an ordinary person dies, the nearest relatives lay the corpse in a cart and take it round to visit their friends. The various families in turn entertain their guests to a meal, and serve the corpse with food just like the rest. The round of visits lasts forty days, and then the body is buried. After a burial the Scythians go through a process of cleaning themselves; they wash their heads with soap, and their bodies in a vapour-bath, the nature of which I will describe. First, however, I must mention that hemp grows in Scythia, a plant resembling flax, but much coarser and taller. It grows wild as well as under cultivation, and the Thracians make clothes from it very like linen ones—indeed, one must have much experience in these matters to be able to distinguish between the two, and anybody who has never seen a piece of cloth made from hemp, will suppose it to be of linen. And now for the vapour-bath: on a framework of three sticks, meeting at the top, they stretch pieces of woollen cloth, taking care to get the joins as perfect as they can, and inside this little tent they put a dish with red-hot stones in it. Then they take some hemp seed, creep into the tent, and throw the seed on to the hot stones. At once it begins to smoke, giving off a vapour unsurpassed by any vapour-bath one could find in Greece. The Scythians enjoy it so much that they howl with pleasure. This is their substitute for an ordinary bath in water, which they never use. The women grind up cypress, cedar, and frankincense on a rough stone, mix the powder into a thick paste with a little water, and plaster it all over their bodies and faces. They leave it on for a day, and then, when they remove it, their skin is clean, glossy, and fragrant.

Like the Egyptians, the Scythians are dead-set against foreign ways, especially against Greek ways. An illustration of this is what happened to Anacharsis—and, later, to Scylas. The former was a great traveller, and a man of great and varied knowledge; he had given proof of this in many parts of the world, and was on his way home to Scythia when, as he was passing through the Hellespont, he broke his journey at Cyzicus. Finding the people of this town engaged in celebrating a magnificent festival in honour of the Mother of the Gods, Anacharsis made a vow that, if he got home safe and sound, he would himself celebrate a night-festival and offer sacrifice to this goddess in exactly the same way as he had seen it done at Cyzicus. On his arrival in Sycthia, he entered the Woodland—that forest of all sorts of trees, which lies near Achilles' Racecourse—and, according to his promise, went through the ceremony with all the proper rites and observances, drum in hand and the images fastened to his dress. He happened to be noticed by some Scythian or other, who at once went and told Saulius, the king; Saulius then came in person, and, seeing Anacharsis occupied with these outlandish rites, shot him dead. To-day, if anyone asks about Anacharsis, the Scythians say they never heard of him—all because he travelled abroad into Greece and adopted foreign practices. But as I was told by Tymnes, the agent of Ariapithes, Anacharsis was the uncle of the Scythian king

Idanthyrsus, and son of Gnurus, grandson of Lycus, and great-grandson of Spargapithes. If he was really a member of this family, he must have been killed by his own brother; for Idanthyrus was a son of Saulius, and it was Saulius who shot him. There is also a different story about Anacharsis which I have heard in the Peloponnese; according to this, he was sent abroad by the king of Scythia to find out what he could about Greece, and told the king on his return that all the Greeks were too busy to study any branch of learning, with the sole exception of the Lacedaemonians, who were the only ones to be able to keep up a sensible conversation. This story, however, is only a frivolous Greek invention; the plain truth is that Anacharsis was killed in the way I have described, for associating with Greeks and adopting foreign ways.

Many years later Scylas came to grief in a similar manner. He was one of the sons of the Scythian king Ariapithes, and his mother, who was not a native woman but came from Istria, taught him to speak and read Greek. As time went on, Ariapithes was treacherously murdered by Spargapithes, the king of the Agathyrsi, and Scylas succeeded to the throne and married Opoea, one of his father's wives. This woman was a native of Scythia, and Ariapithes had a son by her, named Oricus. During his reign, Scylas, as a result of the education his mother had given him, found himself discontented with the traditional way of life in Scythia, and powerfully attracted by Greek ideas. Whenever, therefore, he went with his army to the Greek settlement of the Borysthenites—these people claim to have come originally from Miletus—his custom was to leave his men outside the wall and enter the town himself. Then, when the gates were barred behind him, and the townspeople on the watch to prevent any of the Scythians seeing what he was up to, he would change into Greek clothes, stroll about the streets without any sort of bodyguard or personal attendant, take part in religious ceremonies and behave in every way just as if he were a Greek himself. Often a month or more would go by, before he would change back into his Scythian clothes and leave for home. He was constantly doing this, and even built himself a house there, and married a woman from the neighbourhood to look after it for him. Fate, however, had its revenge in store, as the sequel will show. It happened one day that Scylas conceived the desire to be initiated into the mysteries of Dionysus, and just as he was on the point of beginning the ritual, a terrible thing occurred: the house I mentioned, which he had built—it was a very large and expensive building, set about with marble sphinxes and griffins—was struck from heaven by a thunderbolt and burnt to the ground. In spite of this, however, Scylas carried through the ceremony of initiation.

Now the Greek custom of indulging in Dionysiac orgies is, in Scythian eyes, a shameful thing; and no Scythian can see sense in imagining a god who drives people out of their wits. On this occasion, therefore, at the initiation of Scylas, one of the Borysthenites slipped away and told the Scythians, who were waiting outside the town, of what was going on. 'You laugh at us,' he said, 'for being possessed by the spirit of Dionysus when we celebrate his rites. Well, this same spirit has now taken hold of your own king; he is under its influence—Dionysus has driven him mad. If you don't believe it, come along and I will let you see for yourselves.' The chief Scythians present accepted the offer, and the man took them secretly to the top of a high building, from which they could get a good view of what was happening in the streets. Presently a party of revellers came by, with Scylas amongst them; and when the Scythians saw their king in the grip of the Bacchic frenzy, they were profoundly disturbed and, returning to the army, let every man know of the disgraceful spectacle they had witnessed. Later, when Scylas was at home again, the Scythians put themselves under the protection of his brother Octamasades, the son of Teres' daughter, and rose in rebellion, and Scylas himself, when he learnt what was afoot and understood the reason for it, fled the country and took refuge in Thrace. Octamasades started in pursuit at the head of an army, and made contact with the Thracian forces on the Ister; but before the battle could begin, Sitalces sent a message in the following terms: 'There is really no need for us to begin hostilities. You are my sister's son, and my brother is with you' (this, I should mention, was the truth: Sitalces' brother had fled from Thrace and was living with Octamasades). 'Give me back my brother, and I will do the same with Scylas; then neither of us need risk his army in an engagement.' Octamasades agreed to the proposal and the exchange was effected, whereupon Sitalces went off with his brother, and Octamasades, there and then, had Scylas beheaded. These two stories will show the importance which the Scythians attach to their national traditions, and the severity of the punishments they inflict upon anyone who introduces alien customs.

I was never able to learn exactly what the population of Scythia is. The reports I have heard are not consistent, some putting it very high, others comparatively low—considering, that is, the power and importance of Scythia. They did, however, actually show me something, which gave me a notion of their numbers: between the rivers Borysthenes and Hypanis there is a place called Exampaeus, which I mentioned a little further back in connexion with the salt spring which rises there and makes the water of the Hypanis undrinkable. In this place there stands a brazen bowl, six times as big as the one which was set up as a dedicatory offering at the entrance to the Black Sea by Pausanias, son of Cleombrotus. Anyone who has not seen Pausanias' bowl will understand me better if I say that the Scythian bowl can easily hold 5000 gallons and is of metal about four inches thick. The people of the district told me that this huge vessel was made out of arrowheads; for one of their kings, named Ariantes, wishing to know how many men there were in Scythia, gave orders that each of them should bring him a single arrowhead, failure to do so being punishable by death. An enormous number were brought, and Ariantes decided to turn them into something which might serve as a permanent record. The result was the brazen bowl, which he set up at Exampaeus.

Scythia has few really remarkable features, except its rivers, which are more numerous, and bigger, than anywhere else in the world. There is, however, one other interesting thing besides the rivers and the vast extent of the plains—a footprint left by Heracles. The natives show this to visitors on a rock by the river Tyras. It is like a man's footprint, but is three feet long. I must now leave this subject and get back to the story which I set out to tell.

While Darius was preparing his invasion of Scythia, and sending messengers to every part of his dominions with orders to raise troops here, ships there, and labourers somewhere else to work on the bridge over the Bosphorus, his brother Artabanus did his utmost to make him abandon the enterprise, on the ground that the Scythians were such difficult people to get at. Good though the advice was, it had no effect upon Darius; Artabanus stopped trying to persuade him, and Darius completed his preparations and marched from Susa at the head of his army. A Persian named Oeobazus, who had three sons, all of them in the army, asked Darius to let one of them stay behind, and Darius, as if in answer to a modest request from a personal friend, said he would willingly leave all three. Oeobazus, supposing his sons to be excused service, was delighted, but the king ordered his officers to put the three young men to death. So they were indeed left behind—with their throats cut.

Darius continued his march from Susa to Chalcedon on the Bosphorus, where the bridge was, and then took ship and sailed to the Cyanean rocks—those rocks which according to the Greek story used to be constantly changing their position. Here, seated in the temple which stands by the straits, he looked out over the Black Sea—a sight indeed worth seeing. No sea can equal the Black Sea; it is 1380 miles long, and 410 wide in its widest part. Its mouth is half a mile wide, and the length of the Bosphorus, the narrow strait which leads into it (and where the bridge was), is nearly fifteen miles. The Bosphorus joins the Propontis, which is about sixty miles wide and a hundred and seventy long, and runs into the Hellespont, a narrow strait nearly fifty miles long but less than one mile wide. The Hellespont leads into the broad sea we call the Aegean. The foregoing measurements were arrived at in the following way: in a summer day a ship can cover a distance of approximately 70,000 fathoms, and in a night 60,000. To sail from the entrance of the Black Sea to Phasis— which represents a voyage along its greatest length—takes nine days and eight nights; this would make a distance of 1,110,000 fathom s, or 11,100 furlongs. Across the broadest part, from Sindica to Themiscyra on the Thermodon, it is a voyage of three days and two nights; this comes to 330,000 fathoms, or 3300 furlongs.

. . . I have now given the measurements—and the method of arriving at them— of the Black Sea, Bosphorus, and Hellespont; it remains to add that the Black Sea is connected with a lake nearly as big as itself, called Maeotis, or Mother of the Pontus.

When he had looked on the waters of the Black Sea, Darius returned by ship to the bridge, which had been designed by a Samian named Mandrocles. Then, after seeing what he could of the Bosphorus, he had two marble columns erected, on one of which was an inscription in Assyrian characters showing the various nations which were serving on the campaign; the other had a similar inscription in Greek. These nations were, in fact, all over which he had dominion, and made a total force, including cavalry but excluding the naval contingent, of 700,000 men. There were 600 ships. Years afterwards the people of Byzantium removed these columns and used them in their own city to build the altar of Artemis the Protectress; a single plinth, however, covered with Assyrian characters, was left lying near the temple of Dionysus in Byzantium. I imagine, though I do not know for certain, that Darius' bridge was half-way between Byzantium and the temple which stands on the strait between the Bosphorus and the Black Sea.

Darius was so pleased with the bridge that he loaded its designer with presents, and Mandrocles spent a certain portion of what he received in having a picture painted, showing the whole process of the bridging of the strait, and Darius himself sitting on his throne, with the army crossing over. This picture he presented as a dedicatory, offering to the temple of Hera, with the following verses inscribed upon it, to serve as a permanent record of his achievement:

> Goddess, accept this gift from Mandrocles,
> Who bridged the Bosphorus' fish-haunted seas.
> His labour, praised by King Darius, won
> Honour for Samos, for himself a crown.

Darius, having rewarded Mandrocles, then crossed over into Europe. Before he went, he gave orders to the Ionians—who, with other Greeks from Aeolia and the Hellespont, were in charge of the fleet—to sail into the Black Sea as far as the

Danube, where they were to bridge the river and await his arrival. The orders were obeyed: the naval contingent, passing through the Cyanean Islands, carried right on to the Danube, sailed up the river for two days as far as the point where the main stream divides, and here built the bridge. Darius, after passing over the Bosphorus bridge, marched through Thrace and stopped for three days at the source of the Tearus, a river which has the local reputation of being the best in the world for its curative properties, especially in cases of scab in both men and horses. It originates in thirty-eight separate springs, some hot, some cold, and all issuing from the same rock, which lies at a spot two days' journey both from Heraeum, near Perinthus, and from Apollonia on the Black Sea. The river is a tributary of the Contadesdus which, in its turn, joins the Agrianes, the two streams subsequently uniting with the Hebrus, which falls into the sea near Aenus.

Darius was so greatly charmed with the Tearus, that he erected another pillar close to its source with this inscription: 'The springs of the Tearus, whose water is the finest in action and noblest in appearance of all rivers, was visited in the course of his march against Scythia by Darius son of Hystaspes, finest in action and noblest in appearance of all men, King of Persia and the whole continent.'

Continuing his march, Darius came to another river, the Artiscus, which flows through the country of the Odrysians. Here he indicated a certain spot where every man in the army was ordered to deposit a stone as he passed by. This was done, with the result that when Darius moved on he left great hills of stones behind him.

Before he reached the Danube, the first people he subdued were the Getae, who believe that they never die. The Thracians of Salmydessus and those who live beyond Apollonia and Mesembria, known as the Scyrmiadae and Nipsaeans, surrendered without fighting; but the Getae, who are the most manly and law-abiding of the Thracian tribes, offered fierce resistance and were at once reduced to slavery. The belief of these people in their immortality takes the following form: they never really die, but every man, when he takes leave of this present life, goes to join Salmoxis, a divine being who is also called by some of them Gebeleizis. Every five years they choose one accordance with my change of plans, guard the bridge with every possible care for its safety. This will be the greatest service you can do me.'

After giving his new orders, Darius pressed on without further delay.

Scythia is divided from us by Thrace, which comes down to the sea. Then the coast sweeps round in a great bend where Scythia begins and the Danube flows eastward into the sea. I will now give some indication of the extent of the Scythian coastline, starting from the Danube: across the Danube eastward, ancient Scythia begins, and continues, with the Black Sea as its southern boundary, as far as the town called Carcinitis. Then, still on the Black Sea, the land runs out in a great mountainous promontory and is inhabited by the Tauri, as far as what is known as the Rugged Chersonese which comes down into the eastern sea, Lake Maeotis. For Scythia is bounded on two sides by two different seas, one to the south, the other to the east, much as Attica is; and the position of the Tauri in Scythia is—if I may compare small things with great—as if the promontory of Sunium from Thoricus to Anaphlystus in Attica projected rather further into the sea and were inhabited by some race other than Athenians. Or, to give a different illustration for the benefit of those who have not sailed along this bit of the Attic coast, it is as if some race other than the present inhabitants were to draw a line between the port of Brundisium and Tarentum in Iapygia, and occupy the promontory to seaward of it. These two examples may suggest many others, where the shape of the land resembles the Tauric peninsula. North of the Tauri, and along the sea-coast to the eastward, is again Scythian territory, as is also the country west of the Cimmerian Bosphorus and Lake Maeotis as far as the river Tanais, which flows into the far corner of the lake. On the landward side Scythia is bounded, starting from the Danube, by the following tribes: first the Agathyrsi, next the Neuri, then the Androphagi, and lastly the Melanchlaeni. In shape it is a square, of which the two sides touch the sea; all four sides are equal, those on the sea and those inland. It is a ten days' journey from the Danube to the Borysthenes, and another ten on to Lake Maeotis, making twenty; and it is also a twenty days' journey inland from the Black Sea to the Melanchlaeni whose territory forms the northern boundary. I reckon a day's journey at 200 furlongs, so the two sides of the square which run inland, and the two transverse ones running east and west, are each 4000 furlongs in length.

The Scythians, after discussing the situation and concluding that by themselves they were unequal to the task of coping with Darius in a straight fight, sent off messengers to their neighbours, whose chieftains had already met and were forming plans to deal with what was evidently a threat to their safety on a very large scale. The conference was attended by the chieftains of the following tribes: the Tauri, Agathyrsi, Neuri, Androphagi, Melanchlaeni, Geloni, Budini, and Sauromatae. It is the custom of the Tauri to sacrifice to the Maiden Goddess all shipwrecked sailors and such Greeks as they happen to capture upon their coasts; their method of sacrifice is, after the preliminary ceremonies, to hit the victim on the head with a club. Some say that they push the victim's body over the edge of the cliff on which their temple stands, and fix the head on a stake; others, while agreeing about the head, say the body is not pushed over the cliff, but buried. The Tauri themselves claim that the goddess to whom these offerings are made is Agamemnon's daughter, Iphigenia. Any one of them who takes a prisoner in war, cuts off his head and carries it home, where he sets it up high over the house on a long pole, generally above the chimney. The heads are supposed to act as guardians of the whole house over which they hang. War and plunder are the sources of this people's livelihood.

The Agathyrsi live in luxury and wear gold on their persons. They have their women in common, so that they may all be brothers and, as members of a single family, be able to live together without jealousy or hatred. In other respects their way of life resembles that of the Thracians.

The Neuri share the customs of Scythia. A generation before the campaign of Darius they were forced to quit their country by snakes, which appeared all over the place in great numbers, while still more invaded them from the uninhabited region to the north, until life became so unendurable that there was nothing for it but to move out, and take up their quarters with the Budini. It appears that these people practise magic; for there is a story current amongst the Scythians and the Greeks in Scythia that once a year every Neurian turns into a wolf for a few days, and then turns back into a man again. I do not believe this tale; but all the same, they tell it, and even swear to the truth of it. The Androphagi are the most savage of men, and have no notion of either law or justice. They are herdsmen without fixed dwellings; their dress is Scythian, their language peculiar to themselves, and they are the only people in this part of the world to eat human flesh. The Melanchlaeni all wear black cloaks—hence their name. In all else they resemble the Scythians. The Budini, a numerous and powerful nation, all have markedly blue-grey eyes and red hair; there is a town in their territory called Gelonus, all built of wood, both dwelling-houses and temples, with a high wooden wall round it, thirty furlongs each way. There are temples here in honour of Greek gods, adorned after the Greek manner with statues, altars, and shrines—though all constructed of wood; a triennial festival, with the appropriate revelry, is held in honour of Dionysus. This is to be accounted for by the fact that the Geloni were originally Greeks, who, driven out of the seaports along the coast, settled amongst the Budini. Their language is still half Scythian, half Greek. The language of the Budini is quite different, as, indeed, is their culture generally: they are a pastoral people who have always lived in this part of the country (a peculiarity of theirs is eating lice), whereas the Geloni cultivate the soil, eat grain, and keep gardens, and resemble them neither in appearance nor complexion. In spite of these facts the Greeks lump the Budini and Geloni together under the name of the latter; but they are wrong to do so.

The country here is forest with trees of all sorts. In the most densely wooded part there is a big lake surrounded by reedy marshland; otters and beavers are caught in the lake, and another sort of creature with a square face, whose skin they use for making edgings for their jackets; its testicles are good for affections of the womb.

About the Sauromatae there is the following story. In the war between the Greeks and the Amazons, the Greeks, after their victory at the river Thermodon, sailed off in three ships with as many Amazons on board as they had succeeded in taking alive. (The Scythians call the Amazons *Oeorpata*, the equivalent of *mankillers*, *oeor* being the Scythian word for 'man', and *pata* for 'kill'.) Once at sea, the women murdered their captors, but, as they had no knowledge of boats and were unable to handle either rudder or sail or oar, they soon found themselves, when the men were done for, at the mercy of wind and wave, and were blown to Cremni—the Cliffs—on Lake Maeotis, a place within the territory of the free Scythians. Here they got ashore and made their way inland to an inhabited part of the country. The first thing they fell in with was a herd of horses grazing; these they seized, and, mounting on their backs, rode off in search of loot. The Scythians could not understand what was happening and were at a loss to know where the marauders had come from, as their dress, speech, and nationality were strange to them. Thinking, however, that they were young men, they fought in defence of their property, and discovered from the bodies which came into their possession after the battle that they were women. The discovery gave a new direction to their plans; they decided to make no further attempt to kill the invaders, but to send out a detachment of their youngest men, about equal in number to the Amazons, with orders to camp near them and take their cue from whatever it was that the Amazons then did: if they pursued them, they were not to fight, but to give ground; then, when the pursuit was abandoned, they were once again to encamp within easy range. The motive behind this policy was the Scythians' desire to get children by the Amazons. The detachment of young men obeyed their orders, and the Amazons, realizing that they meant no harm, did not attempt to molest them, with the result that every day the two camps drew a little closer together. Neither party had anything but their weapons and their horses, and both lived the same sort of life, hunting and plundering.

Towards midday the Amazons used to scatter and go off to some little distance in ones and twos to ease themselves, and the Scythians, when they noticed this, followed suit; until one of them, coming upon an Amazon girl all by herself, began to make advances to her. She, nothing loth, gave him what he wanted, and then told him by signs (being unable to express her meaning in words, as neither understood the other's language) to return on the following day with a friend, making it clear that there must be two men, and that she herself would bring another girl. The young man then left her and told the others what had happened, and on the next day took a friend to the same spot, where he found his Amazon waiting for him and another one with her. Having learnt of their success, the rest of the young Scythians soon succeeded in getting the Amazons to submit to their wishes. The two camps were then united, and Amazons and Scythians lived together, every man keeping as his wife the woman whose favours he had first enjoyed. The men could not learn the women's language, but the women succeeded in picking up the men's; so when they could understand one another, the Scythians made the following proposal: 'We', they said, 'have parents and property. Let us give up our present way of life and return to live with our people. We will keep you as our wives and not take any others.' The Amazons replied: 'We and the women of your nation could never live together; our ways are too much at variance. We are riders; our business is with the bow and the spear, and we know nothing of women's work; but in your country no woman has anything to do with such things—your women stay at home in their waggons occupied with feminine tasks, and never go out to hunt or for any other purpose. We could not possibly agree. If, however, you wish to keep us for your wives and to behave as honourable men, go and get from your parents the share of property which is due to you, and then let us go off and live by ourselves.' The young men agreed to this, and when they came back, each with his portion of the family possessions, the Amazons said: 'We dread the prospect of settling down here, for we have done much damage to the country by our raids, and we have robbed you of your parents. Look now—if you think fit to keep us for your wives, let us get out of the country altogether and settle somewhere on the other side of the Tanais.' Once again the Scythians agreed, so they crossed the Tanais and travelled east for three days, and then north, for another three, from Lake Maeotis, until they reached the country where they are to-day, and settled down there. Ever since then the women of the Sauromatae have kept to their old ways, riding to the hunt on horseback sometimes with, sometimes without, their menfolk, taking part in war and wearing the same sort of clothes as men. The language of these people is the Scythian, but it has always been a corrupt form of it because the Amazons were never able to learn to speak it properly. They have a marriage law which forbids a girl to marry until she has killed an enemy in battle; some of their women, unable to fulfil this condition, grow old and die in spinsterhood.

These, then, were the nations whose chieftains had met together to discuss the common danger; and to them the envoys from Scythia brought the news that the Persian king, having overrun the whole of the other continent, had bridged the Bosphorus and crossed into Europe, where he had already brought Thrace into subjection and was now engaged in throwing a bridge across the Danube, with the intention of making himself master of all Europe too. 'We beg you,' they said, 'not to remain neutral in this struggle; do not let us be destroyed without raising a hand to help us. Let us rather form a common plan of action, and meet the invader together. If you refuse, we shall be forced to yield to pressure and either abandon our country or make terms with the enemy. Without your help, what else could we do? What will become of us? Moreover, if you stand aside, you will not on that account get out of things any more lightly; for this invasion is aimed at you just as much as at us, and, once we have gone under, the Persians will never be content to leave you unmolested. There is plain proof of the truth of this: for had the Persian attack been directed against us alone in revenge for the old wrong we did them when we enslaved their country, they would have been bound to come straight for Scythia without touching any other nation on the way. By doing that they would have made it plain to everyone that the object of their attack was Scythia, and Scythia alone; but, as things are, they no sooner crossed into Europe than they have begun to bring under their heel in turn every nation through whose territory they pass. Not to mention the other Thracians, even our neighbours the Getae have been enslaved.'

The assembled chieftains deliberated upon what the Scythian envoys had reported, but failed to reach a unanimous conclusion. Those of the Geloni, Budini, and Sauromatae agreed to stand by the Scythians, but the rest—the chieftains, namely, of the Agathyrsi, Neuri, Androphagi, Melanchlaeni, and Tauri—returned the following answer. 'Had you not yourselves been the aggressors in your trouble with Persia, we should have considered your request justified; we should have granted what you ask and been willing enough to fight at your side. But the fact is, you invaded Persia without consulting us, and remained in possession of it as long as heaven allowed you, and now the same power is urging the Persians to pay you back in your own coin. We did the Persians no injury on that former occasion, and we will not be the first to start trouble now. Of course, should they prove to be the aggressors and actually invade us, we shall do our best to keep them out; but until we see that happen, we will stay where we are and do nothing. In our opinion, the invasion is directed not against us, but against you, who were the aggressor in the first place.'

When this reply was reported to the Scythians, seeing that these nations refused to support them, they decided to avoid a straight fight, and to retire, blocking up all the wells and springs which they passed and trampling the pasture. They organized their forces in two divisions. One, under the command of Scopasis, was to be joined by the Sauromatae, and had orders if the Persians turned against them to withdraw along the coast of Lake Maeotis toward the river Don, and, should the Persians themselves retreat, to attack them in their turn. This was one division, and this was the route it was to take. Of the other, the two sections—the greater under Idanthyrsus and the second under Taxacis—were to unite forces and, after joining up with the Geloni and Budini, were, like the first division, to withdraw before the Persian advance at the distance of a day's march, and carry out as they went the same strategy. This division was to begin by retiring in the direction of those nations who had refused to join the alliance, with the idea of involving them in the war against their will, if they would not fight on their own initiative. Subsequently, this second force was to go back to their own country and launch an attack, if the situation seemed to justify it.

Having determined on this plan of action, the Scythians marched out to meet Darius, sending their best horsemen in advance. The waggons which served as houses for the women and children, and all the cattle, except what they needed for food, were ordered to move northward at once, in advance of their future line of retreat. The advance-guard made contact with the Persians about three days' march from the Danube, and at once encamped at a distance of a single day's march in front of them, devastating the land. The Persians, on the appearance of the Scythian cavalry, gave chase and continued to follow in their tracks as they withdrew before them. The Persian advance was now directed against the single division of the Scythian army under Scopasis, and was consequently eastward towards the Don. The Scythians crossed the river, and the Persians followed in pursuit, until they had passed through the territory of the Sauromatae and reached that of the Budini, where they came across the wooden fortified town of Gelonus, abandoned and empty of defenders, and burnt it. Previously, so long as their route lay through the country of the Scythians and Sauromatae, they had done no damage, because the country was barren and there was nothing to destroy. After burning the town, they continued to press forward on the enemy's heels, until they reached the great uninhabited region which lies beyond the territory of the Budini. This tract of land is seven days' journey across, and on the further side of it lies the country of the Thyssagetae, from which four great rivers, Lycus, Oarus, Tanais, and Syrgis, flow through the land of the Maeotae to empty themselves into lake Maeotis.

When he reached this uninhabited area, Darius called a halt on the banks of the Oarus, and began eight large forts, spaced at regular intervals of approximately eight miles. The remains of them were still to be seen in my day. While these forts were under construction, the Scythians whom he had been following changed the direction of their march, and by a broad sweep through the country to the northward returned to Scythia and completely disappeared. Unable to see any sign of them, Darius left his forts half finished and himself turned back towards the west, supposing that the Scythians he had been chasing were the whole nation, and that they were now trying to escape in that direction. He made the best speed he was capable of, and on reaching Scythia fell in with the other two combined divisions of the Scythian army; at once he gave chase, and they, as before, withdrew a day's march in front of him. As Darius continued to press forward in hot pursuit, the Scythians now carried out their plan of leading him into the territory of the people who had refused, in the first instance, to support them in their resistance to Persia. The first were the Melanchlaeni, and the double invasion of their country, first by the Scythians and then by the Persians, caused great disturbance; the turn of the Androphagi came next, and then the Neuri, with the same result. Finally, still withdrawing before the Persian advance, the Scythians approached the frontiers of the Agathyrsi. These people, unlike their neighbours, of whose terrified attempt to escape they had been witness, did not wait for the Scythians to invade them, but sent a representative to forbid them to cross the frontier, adding a warning that, if they attempted to do so, they would be resisted by force of arms. This challenge they followed up by manning their frontiers in arms. The other tribes—the Melanchlaeni, Androphagi, and Neuri—offered no resistance to the successive invasions of Scythians and Persians, but forgot their former threats and in great confusion fled northwards into the waste. The Scythians, finding the Agathyrsi prepared to keep them out, then changed direction, and, from the land of the Neuri, drew the Persians back into Scythia.

Finding no end of this, Darius at last dispatched a rider with a message for Idanthyrsus, the Scythian king. 'Why on earth, my good sir,' the message ran, 'do you keep on running away? You have, surely, a choice of two alternatives: if you think yourself strong enough to oppose me, stand up and fight, instead of wandering all over the world in your efforts to escape me; or, if you admit that you are too weak, what is the good, even so, of running away? You should rather send earth and water to your master, as the sign of your submission, and come to a conference.'

'Persian,' Idanthyrsus replied, 'I have never yet run from any man fear; and I am not doing so now from you. There is, for me, nothing unusual in what I have been doing: it is precisely the sort of life I always lead, even in times of peace. If you want to know why I will not fight, I will tell you: in our country there are no towns and no cultivated land; fear of losing which, or seeing it ravaged, might indeed provoke us to hasty battle. If, however, you are determined upon bloodshed with the least possible delay, one thing there is for which we will fight—the tombs of our forefathers. Find those tombs, and try to wreck them, and you will soon know whether or not we are willing to stand up to you. Till then—unless for good reason—we shall continue to avoid a battle. This is my reply to your challenge; and as for your being my master, I acknowledge no masters but Zeus from whom I sprang, and Hestia the

Scythian queen. I will send you no gifts of earth and water, but others more suitable; and your claim to be my master is easily answered—be dammed to you!' This was the message which was carried back to Darius.

Study Questions

1. What did Scythians offer as sacrifices to their gods? Were there ever human sacrifices? What would the Scythians never offer in sacrifice?

2. What were the customs for the first man a Scythian warrior killed? With subsequent victims?

3. What did the Scythians do with the worst of their enemies?

4. What did Scythian soothsayers work with?

5. How did the Scythians conclude oaths or solemn compacts?

6. How were the bodies of dead Scythian kings prepared?

7. How did the Scythians bathe themselves?

8. What strange way of reckoning the population of Scythia does Herodotus describe?

9. Herodotus describes a meeting of tribes for the purpose of formulating strategy against Darius and the Persians. He then goes off on a tangent about the customs of these various tribes. What does he say about an encounter between a Scythian group and the Amazons?

10. The Scythians appealed to other tribes to form common action against the Persians. Some tribes accepted this, but others rejected the alliance. Why the rejection?

11. How did the Scythians "sucker," so to speak, the armies of Darius into a dangerous position?

12. Finding Scythian military tactics exasperating, Darius wrote a letter to Idanthyrsus, the Scythian king. What did he say in this letter? What was Idanthrysus's reply?

III.

The Hsiung-nu

The Hsiung-nu were a warlike pastoral nomadic people who inhabited the steppe regions north of China. They were known to the Chinese several centuries before the birth of Christ, but by the second century B.C. they had built a huge steppe empire that threatened the security of China's Han dynasty (202 B.C.–A.D. 220). Han China agreed to marry off Han royal princesses to Hsiung-nu leaders as a way of maintaining peace, but by the first century B.C. a more powerful China cancelled the intermarriage arrangements and insisted on a new framework of foreign relations, the "tribute system," which the Hsiung-nu ultimately and reluctantly accepted. By the first century A.D. the Hsiung-nu attacked and menaced China once again. Ultimately subjugated once more by the Chinese during the late first century, the Hsiung-nu nonetheless remained a force to be reckoned with north of China for several more centuries.

Controversy still rages about the connection, in whatever terms conceived, between the Hsiung-nu and the Huns known to the Europeans. The ethnonyms "Hun" and "Hsiung-nu" are almost certainly related, and both the Huns and Hsiung-nu were certainly pastoral nomadic warriors. In the 1750s a French Orientalist proposed the identity of the Hsiung-nu with the Huns, and his identification has been hotly debated ever since. Today the debate is primarily between two energetic Hungarian scholars: Dr. Miklós Érdy, who affirms it, and Prof. Dr. Denis Sinor, who denies it. I have written a history of this long and involved debate.[2]

---

2. David Curtis Wright, "The Hsiung-nu—Hun Equation Revisited," *Eurasian Studies Yearbook* 69 (1997): 77–112.

A. Ssu-ma Ch'ien/Sima Qian

Su-ma Ch'ien (c. 145–85 B.C.; also spelled Sima Qian) is China's greatest historian. He is at once China's Herodotus and Thucydides. His monumental *Shih-chi* ("Records of the Grand Historian") is a comprehensive history of China, drawing as it does on available historical materials and traditions from remotest antiquity to Ssu-ma Ch'ien's own day. Its organization, which included chronological and topical formats, established the model for all subsequent Chinese historical writing. Ssu-ma Ch'ien's father served as Grand Astrologer in the Han government, and this began his family's involvement in record keeping. With access to many kinds of historical documents, Ssu-ma Ch'ien's father began work on the *Shih-chi*. Ssu-ma Ch'ien succeeded formally to his father's position in 105 B.C., three years after his father's death. During his service in this capacity, Ssu-ma Ch'ien assumed his father's official duties and also his work on the *Shih-chi*.

Tragedy struck Ssu-ma Ch'ien in 99 B.C. He defended the reputation of a Han general who was defeated and captured by the Hsiung-nu. The Han emperor Wu-ti (r. 140–87 B.C.) became so enraged at Ssu-ma Ch'ien's stubborn defense of the general's honor that he had him imprisoned. Ssu-ma Ch'ien was eventually convicted of the crime of *lesè majesté* and sentenced to death. His family's penurious circumstances would not permit his monetary redemption, so he had three choices: execution, suicide, or the alternative but extremely distressing punishment of castration. He ultimately chose castration, longing to fulfil his filial duty of completing his father's history. Unable to produce a male heir, Ssu-ma Ch'ien channelled his paternal instincts into the writing of history, which he did with conscientiousness and extraordinary dedication. His great history is the posterity he bequeathed to subsequent generations.

The passages excerpted here on the Hsiung-nu are from Chapter 110, the single largest and most important source on the Hsiung-nu now available.

Shih chi 110
The Account of the Hsiung-nu
Ssu-ma Ch'ien

From the time of the Three Dynasties on, the Hsiung-nu have been a source of constant worry and harm to China. The Han has attempted to determine the Hsiung-nu's periods of strength and weakness so that it may adopt defensive measures or launch punitive expeditions as the circumstances allow. Thus I made The Account of the Hsiung-nu.

The ancestor of the Hsiung-nu was a descendant of the rulers of the Hsia dynasty by the name of Ch'un-wei. As early as the time of Emperors Yao and Shun and before, we hear of these people, known as Mountain Barbarians, Hsien-yün, or Hun-chu, living in the region of the northern barbarians and wandering from place to place pasturing their animals. The animals they raise consist mainly of horses, cows, and sheep, but include such rare beasts as camels, asses, mules, and the wild horses known as *t'ao-t'u* and *t'o-chi*. They move about in search of water and pasture and have no walled cities or fixed dwellings, nor do they engage in any kind of agriculture. Their lands, however, are divided into regions under the control of various leaders.

They have no writing, and even promises and agreements are only verbal. The little boys start out by learning to ride sheep and shoot birds and rats with a bow and arrow, and when they get a little older they shoot foxes and hares, which are used for food. Thus all the young men are able to use a bow and act as armed cavalry in time of war. It is their custom to herd their flocks in times of peace and make their living by hunting, but in periods of crisis they take up arms and go off on plundering and marauding expeditions. This seems to be their inborn nature. For long-range weapons they use bows and arrows, and swords and spears at close range. If the battle is going well for them they will advance, but if not, they will retreat, for they do not consider it a disgrace to run away. Their only concern is self-advantage, and they know nothing of propriety or righteousness.

From the chiefs of the tribe on down, everyone eats the meat of the domestic animals and wears clothes of hide or wraps made of felt or fur. The young men eat the richest and best food, while the old get what is left over, since the tribe honors those who are young and strong and despises the weak and aged. On the death of his father, a son will marry his stepmother, and when brothers die, the remaining brothers will take the widows for their own wives. They have no polite names but only personal names, and they observe no taboos in the use of personal names.

. . . At this time the Eastern Barbarians were very powerful and the Yüeh-chih were likewise flourishing. The *Shan-yü* or chieftain of the Hsiung-nu was named T'ou-man. T'ou-man, unable to hold out against the Ch'in forces, had withdrawn to the far north, where he lived with his subjects for over ten years. After Meng T'ien died and the feudal lords revolted against the Ch'in, plunging China into a period of strife and turmoil, the convicts which the Ch'in had sent to the northern border to garrison the area all returned to their homes. The Hsiung-nu, the pressure against them relaxed, once again began to infiltrate south of the bend of the Yellow River until they had established themselves along the old border of China.

T'ou-man's oldest son, the heir apparent to his position, was named Mo-tun, but the *Shan-yü* also had a younger son by another consort whom he had taken later and was very fond of. He decided that he wanted to get rid of Mo-tun and set up his younger son as heir instead, and he therefore sent Mo-tun as a hostage to the Yüeh-chih nation. Then, after Mo-tun had arrived among the Yüeh-chih, T'ou-man made a sudden attack on them. The Yüeh-chih were about to kill Mo-tun in retaliation, but he managed to steal one of their best horses and escape, eventually making his way back home. His father, struck by his bravery, put him in command of a force of ten thousand cavalry.

Mo-tun had some arrows made that whistled in flight and used them to drill his troops in shooting from horseback. "Shoot wherever you see my whistling arrow strike!" he ordered, "and anyone who fails to shoot will be cut down!" Then he went out hunting for birds and animals, and if any of his men failed to shoot at what he himself had shot at, he cut them down on the spot. After this, he shot a whistling arrow at one of his best horses. Some of his men hung back and did not dare shoot at the horse, whereupon Mo-tun at once executed them. A little later he took an arrow and shot at his favorite wife. Again some of his men shrank back in terror and failed to discharge their arrows, and again he executed them on the spot. Finally he went out hunting with his men and shot a whistling arrow at one of his father's finest horses. All his followers promptly discharged their arrows in the same direction, and Mo-tun knew that at last they could be trusted. Accompanying his father, the *Shan-yü* T'ou-man, on a hunting expedition, he shot a whistling arrow at his father and every one of his followers aimed their arrows in the same direction and shot the *Shan-yü* dead. Then Mo-tun executed his stepmother, his younger brother, and all the high officials of the nation who refused to take orders from him, and set himself up as the new *Shan-yü*.

At this time the Eastern Barbarians were very powerful and, hearing that Mo-tun had killed his father and made himself leader, they sent an envoy to ask if they could have T'ou-man's famous horse that could run a thousand *li* in one day. Mo-tun consulted his ministers, but they all replied, "The thousand-*li* horse is one of the treasures of the Hsiung-nu people. You should not give it away!"

"When a neighboring country asks for it, why should I begrudge them one horse?" he said, and sent them the thousand-*li* horse.

After a while the Eastern Barbarians, supposing that Mo-tun was afraid of them, sent an envoy to ask for one of Mo-tun's consorts. Again Mo-tun questioned his ministers, and they replied in a rage, "The Eastern Barbarians are unreasoning beasts to come and request one of the *Shan-yü's* consorts. We beg to attack them!"

But Mo-tun replied, "If it is for a neighboring country, why should I begrudge them one woman?" and he sent his favorite consort to the Eastern Barbarians.

With this the ruler of the Eastern Barbarians grew more and more bold and arrogant, invading the lands to the west. Between his territory and that of the Hsiung-nu was an area of over a thousand *li* of uninhabited land; the two peoples made their homes on either side of this wasteland. The ruler of the Eastern Barbarians sent an envoy to Mo-tun saying, "The Hsiung-nu have no way of using this stretch of wasteland which lies between my border and yours. I would like to take possession of it!"

When Mo-tun consulted his ministers, some of them said; "Since the land is of no use you might as well give it to him," while others said, "No, you must not give it away!"

Mo-tun flew into a rage. "Land is the basis of the nation!" he said. "Why should I give it away?" And he executed all the ministers who had advised him to do so.

Then he mounted his horse and set off to attack the Eastern Barbarians, circulating an order throughout his domain that anyone who was slow to follow would be executed. The Eastern Barbarians had up until this time despised Mo-tun and made no preparations for their defense; when Mo-tun and his soldiers arrived, they inflicted a crushing defeat, killing the ruler of the Eastern Barbarians, taking prisoner his subjects, and seizing their domestic animals. Then he returned and rode west, attacking and routing the Yüeh-chih, and annexed the lands of the ruler of Lou-fan and the ruler of Po-yang south of the Yellow River. Thus he recovered possession of all the lands which the Ch'in general Meng T'ien had taken away from the Hsiung-nu; the border between his territory and that of the Han empire now followed the old line of defenses south of the Yellow River, and from there he marched into the Ch'ao-na and Fu-shih districts and then invaded Yen and Tai.

At this time the Han forces were stalemated in battle with the armies of Hsiang Yü, and China was exhausted by warfare. Thus Mo-tun was able to strengthen his position, massing a force of over three hundred thousand skilled crossbowmen.

Over a thousand years had elapsed from the time of Ch'un-wei, the ancestor of the Hsiung-nu, to that of Mo-tun, a vast period during which the tribes split up and scattered into various groups, sometimes expanding, sometimes dwindling in size. Thus it is impossible to give any ordered account of the lineage of the Hsiung-nu rulers. When Mo-tun came to power, however, the Hsiung-nu reached their peak of strength and size, subjugating all of the other barbarian tribes of the north and turning south to confront China as an enemy nation.

. . . In the first month of the year the various leaders come together in a small meeting at the *Shan-yü's* court to perform sacrifices, and in the fifth month a great meeting is held at Lung-ch'eng at which sacrifices are conducted to the Hsiung-nu ancestors, Heaven and Earth, and the gods and spirits. In the autumn, when the horses are fat, another great meeting is held at the Tai Forest when a reckoning is made of the number of persons and animals.

According to Hsiung-nu law, anyone who in ordinary times draws his sword a foot from the scabbard is condemned to death. Anyone convicted of theft has his property confiscated. Minor offenses are punished by flogging and major ones by death. No one is kept in jail awaiting sentence longer than ten days, and the number of imprisoned men for the whole nation does not exceed a handful.

At dawn the *Shan-yü* leaves his camp and makes obeisance to the sun as it rises, and in the evening he makes a similar obeisance to the moon. In seating arrangements the left side or the seat facing north is considered the place of honor. The days *wu* and *chi* of the ten-day week are regarded as most auspicious.

In burials the Hsiung-nu use an inner and an outer coffin, with accessories of gold, silver, clothing, and fur, but they do not construct grave mounds or plant trees on the grave, nor do they use mourning garments. When a ruler dies, the ministers and concubines who were favored by him and who are obliged to follow him in death often number in the hundreds or even thousands.

Whenever the Hsiung-hu begin some undertaking, they observe the stars and the moon. They attack when the moon is full and withdraw their troops when it wanes. After a battle those who have cut off the heads of the enemy or taken prisoners are presented with a cup of wine and allowed to keep the spoils they have captured. Any prisoners that are taken are made slaves. Therefore, when they fight, each man strives for his own gain. They are very skillful at using decoy troops to lure their opponents to destruction. When they catch sight of the enemy, they swoop down like a flock of birds, eager for booty, but when they find themselves hard pressed and beaten, they scatter and vanish like the mist. Anyone who succeeds in recovering the body of a comrade who has fallen in battle receives all of the dead man's property.

. . . When one of the Han envoys to the Hsiung-nu remarked scornfully that Hsiung-nu custom showed no respect for the aged, Chung-hsing Shuo began to berate him. "According to Han custom," he said, "when the young men are called into military service and sent off with the army to garrison the frontier, do not their old parents at home voluntarily give up their warm clothing and tasty food so that there will be enough to provide for the troops?"

"Yes, they do," admitted the Han envoy.

"The Hsiung-nu make it clear that warfare is their business. And since the old and the weak are not capable of fighting, the best food and drink are naturally allotted to the young men in the prime of life. So the young men are willing to fight for the defense of the nation, and both fathers and sons are able to live out their lives in security. How can you say that the Hsiung-nu despise the aged?"

"But among the Hsiung-nu," the envoy continued, "fathers and sons sleep together in the same tent. And when a father dies, the sons marry their own stepmothers, and when brothers die, their remaining brothers marry their widows! These people know nothing of the elegance of hats and girdles, nor of the rituals of the court!"

"According to Hsiung-nu custom," replied Chung-hsing Shuo, "the people eat the flesh of their domestic animals, drink their milk, and wear their hides, while the animals graze from place to place, searching for pasture and water. Therefore, in wartime the men practice riding and shooting, while in times of peace they enjoy themselves and have nothing to do. Their laws are simple and easy to carry out; the relation between ruler and subject is relaxed and intimate, so that the governing of the whole nation is no more complicated than the governing of one person. The reason that sons marry their stepmothers and brothers marry their widowed sisters-in-law is simply that they hate to see the clan die out. Therefore, although the Hsiung-nu encounter times of turmoil, the ruling families always manage to stand firm. In China, on the other hand, though a man would never dream of marrying his stepmother or his brother's widow, yet the members of the same family drift so far apart that they end up murdering each other! This is precisely why so many changes of dynasty have come about in China! Moreover, among the Chinese, as etiquette and the sense of duty decay, enmity arises between the rulers and the ruled, while the excessive building of houses and dwellings exhausts the strength and resources of the nation. Men try to get their food and clothing by farming and raising silkworms and to insure their safety by building walls and fortifications. Therefore, although danger threatens, the Chinese people are given no training in aggressive warfare, while in times of stability they must still wear themselves out trying to make a living. Pooh! You people in your mud huts—you talk too much! Enough of this blabbering and mouthing! Just because you wear hats, what does that make you?"

After this, whenever the Han envoys would try to launch into any sermons or orations, Chung-hsing Shuo would cut them off at once. "Not so much talk from the

Han envoys! Just make sure that the silks and grainstuffs you bring to the Hsiung-nu are of the right measure and quality, that's all. What's the need for talking? If the goods you deliver are up to measure and of good quality, all right. But if there is any deficiency or the quality is no good, then when the autumn harvest comes we will take our horses and trample all over your crops!"

Day and night he instructed the *Shan-yü* on how to maneuver into a more advantageous position.

Study Questions

1. What animals did the Hsiung-nu herd?
2. Why did the Hsiung-nu move about, according to Ssu-ma Ch'ien?
3. What did little Hsiung-nu boys learn to do?
4. What, according to Ssu-ma Ch'ien, was the "inborn nature" of the Hsiung-nu?
5. What did the Hsiung-nu not consider a disgrace?
6. In a few sentences, tell how Mo-tun overcame his father, T'ou-man, to become *shan-yü* (leader or khan) of the Hsiung-nu.
7. Why did Mo-tun attack the Eastern Barbarians? Was he successful in this attack?
8. What particular Hsiung-nu religious practice does Ssu-ma Ch'ien mention?
9. Ssu-ma Ch'ien describes the revulsion that a Han envoy felt at Hsiung-nu society. How did the Hsiung-nu named Chung-hsing Shuo respond? Did he have much respect for Han Chinese society? What is the one thing he asked (required, really) of the Han?

B. Hou Han shu

The *Hou Han shu* ("History of the Later Han") by Fan Yeh (A.D. 398–445) covers the Han dynasty from its restoration from a usurper in A.D. 25 to its final downfall in A.D. 220. It follows the same basic format established by Ssu-ma Ch'ien. The passages excerpted from it below pertain to the Hsiung-nu. The translator, the English Sinologist (China specialist) E. H. Parker, accepts the equation of the Hsiung-nu with the Huns known to the Roman Empire and thus renders "Hsiung-nu" as "Huns." These excerpted translations below were published in the late nineteenth century.

Turko-Scythian Tribes
After Han Dynasty
From the *Hou Han shu*

In the 28th year the northern Huns again sent an envoy to the palace with tribute of horses and fur-coats, once more begging for friendly relations, and also for some musicians. They craved permission, besides, to bring all their Tartar allies from Turkestan to do audience duty. The Emperor sent the matter down to the three chief ministers for deliberation as to the best answer to give. One *Pan Piao,* Secretary to one of the ministries, memorialized thus:—'I understand that his Majesty *Süan* of pious memory warned the guardians of the frontier what a great, fickle, and treacherous power the Huns were; and that if they were conciliated by judicious intercourse they would be available for repelling the enemy and bearing the brunt of their attacks, whereas if their calculations were too easily responded to they would turn round and despise you. At the present moment the northern Huns, observing that the southern Huns have joined us, fear a conspiracy against their dominion, and therefore they have made repeated friendly advances, and have driven in their sheep and cattle from a great distance in order to trade with us; they have sent one prince after the other with liberal tribute offerings. This is merely an external exhibition of wealth and power in order to coax us. The heavier their offerings the poorer, I take it, their country really is. The oftener they make friendly advances, the more they fear us. Still, as we have not yet been able to get much assistance out of the south, we ought not to break off entirely with the north. We can not in decency fail to acknowledge the principle of benevolent neutrality. In other words, we may well give them liberal presents, calculated upon the value of what they have offered us; at the same time expounding very clearly to them what they may expect from the precedents of *Hu-han-ya* and *Chï-chï.* If a reply is to be sent which is to have good effect, I submit the following draft:'—

[Here follows the reply which runs thus]:—

'The Khan does not forget the grace of *Han,* and recalls his ancestors' old treaties, being desirous of improving friendly relations with a view to his own personal ease and to the interests of his dominion. The proposition is a very worthy one, and for that reason the Khan has our approval. In past times the Huns underwent a long period of anarchy, *Hu-han-ya* and *Chï-chï* were at feud with each other, but luckily the grace of his majesty Pius *Süan* descended upon them as an *aegis,* and they both of them sent their sons as pages to court and declared themselves border vassals for the protection of the Wall. After that, *Chï-chï* broke with the august favour in a huff, whilst *Hu-han-ya* adhered to his friendly policy and exhibited a further degree of pious loyalty; so when *Han* extinguished *Chï-chï, Hu-han-ya* saved his dominion and passed it on to his sons and grandsons one after the other. Recently the Southern Khan has faced south, and presented himself at the Wall with his horde to receive our commands; and, as he is the oldest direct descendant of *Hu-han-ya,* we have held that the succession is his due. But, in failure of his duty, he has extended his conquests, and has made attacks in a suspicious spirit, craving for troops with a view to securing the submission and disappearance of the Northern horde, involving himself in complications the end of which it is impossible to foresee. We cannot confine ourselves to considering only his side of the question, for we must take into account that the Northern Khan has for successive years offered tribute and expressed a desire to improve relations, in consequence of which we have rejected and disapproved of the Southern Khan's propositions, in order to give effect to the [Northern] Khan's loyal and filial sentiments. *Han* stands, by reason of her prestige and good faith, as the supreme director of the myriad kingdoms: all on whom the sun and moon do shine are her lieges and handmaidens. Though customs may differ among the hundred barbarians, in question of justice, no considerations of remoteness or proximity intervene. Those who submit and obey are rewarded. Those who rebel and resist are punished. Such are the consequences of good or evil; such are the examples of *Hu-han-ya* and *Chï-chï*. Now the Khan wishes to improve friendly relations: his genuine feelings have been manifested. What objection therefore can there be to his conducting all the countries of the Western Regions to come and perform tribute duty? In what does the fact that the States of the Western Regions belong to the Huns, differ from their belonging to *Han?* The Khan has undergone repeated wars and civil commotions: the interior of his dominions must be exhausted. Articles of tribute are after all only the expression of an idea. Why need he offer horses and fur coats? We now send as presents to the Khan 500 pieces of mixed lustrings, a bow, a bow-case, an arrow-case, and four sets of arrows. We also present the *Kuh-tu* marquess and Right *Luh-li* Prince, who offered us some horses, each with 400 pieces of mixed lustrings, a horse, and a scimitar. The Khan said some time ago, that the flutes, harps and harpsichords, presented to *Hu-han-ya* in the time of former Emperors, are all worn out, and he wishes to have them renewed. Remembering that the Khan's State was not at peace, and that he was just working up his military power, when his occupation would consist rather in warlike contests that in fluting and harping, the comparative importance of which to him must be very small, we did not send these articles. But we will not grudge him these insignificant objects, which we send, with this, by ordinary post-messenger for his information.' The Emperor accepted all this in its entirety.

. . . The *Hien-yun* and *Hün-yüh* have been China's enemies from the most ancient times till now. Though there have been periods when friendliness prevailed in name, there has never been the least advantage to us from it, and the out-of-the-way frontier folk have repeatedly had to endure their ravages. Fathers died at the beginning, and sons fought at the end. Delicate females crowded into the guard-stations, and orphan children wept along the roads. Aged mothers and widowed wives set up hopeless altars of prayer and drank their own tears, looking in vain for the return of their dead ones from the desert beyond. Oh! how pitiful! The philosopher *Lao-Tsz* says that one reason why the Great River and the Ocean out-live the smaller streams is because they are below them. What harm can it do to us then to be also a little humble and lowly? And especially now that the Huns are definitely divided amongst themselves. Their language is submissive and the treaties are clear, whilst their tribute offerings come in heaps and piles. How, then, can it be right to break faith and put ourselves in the wrong? *Tu-liao* is hereby ordered, as also is General *P'ang Fén*, to give double rations to all the souls captured by the southern horde, and to return them to the northern freebooters. At the same time the rewards for heads cut off by the southern horde and for captives taken must be paid on the usual scale.

. . . In past times the Emperor *Wu Ti* greatly extended the empire, and was desirous of reducing the Huns to subjection, but, as it did not please Heaven that it should be done then, his wish was not fulfilled. In the time of the Emperor *Süan,* however, *Hu-han-ya* came with his submission, in consequence of which the frontier folk secured peace, and inner and outer became as one, increasing and developing quietly for a period of over sixty years. Then *Wang Mang* usurped the throne, and changed the Khan's official title. Devastating raids were incessant and the Khan rebelled. But when *Kwang wu* received [Heaven's] commands, he once more brought them into the fold, and the recovery of the territory of the frontier prefectures was thus made possible. The *Wu-hwan* and *Sien-pi* were all so impressed that they also reverted to loyalty, while our prestige kept down the western barbarians. Such were the great results. Now, happily, destiny has it that Heaven allows the Northern free-booters to struggle apart. To make use of barbarian to attack barbarian is for the advantage of the republic, and we may well hearken and approve.'

. . . The Huns are well aware of the enormity of their offence in revolting and committing raids. But even birds and beasts will turn at bay in order to escape death. How much more a national horde too numerous for extermination! Our commis-sariat labours are becoming more serious day by day, and the armies are becoming exhausted with the severe demands made upon them. It is not the true interest of China to exhaust the interior for the sake of what is outside. In my humble opinion the *Tu-liao* general *Ma Tsih* has given ample evidence of his strategical abilities, and moreover he has commanded the frontier for a long time, and profoundly under-stands the essential points of warfare. Whenever I receive letters from *Tsih*, I find that his views coincide with mine. *Tsih* should be ordered to hold a strongly fortified posi-tion, and from it negotiate to secure a surrender by the exhibition of kindness and good faith, proclaiming offers of rewards, and explaining their duties to them. In this way the rogues can be subdued, and the State will be freed from trouble.'

The Emperor approved, and commanded *Tsih* to induce the revolted free-booters to surrender. *Shang* also sent letters to *Tsih*, etc., saying:—'China has been at peace so long that she has forgotten how to fight. Chance hand-to-hand encounters with magnificent horsemen are of uncertain result: this is the strong point of the Tartar nomads, and the weak point of China. Strong crossbows fired off from the city walls, solid camps strongly guarded awaiting the attack: this is China's strong point, whilst it is the Tartars' weak point. We ought to confine ourselves in the first instance to what is our strong point, whilst we observe what they are going to do, at the same time offering rewards and proclaiming the advantages of repentance, and not allow-ing ourselves in our eagerness for petty successes to mar the main business in hand.'

Study Questions

1. What did the Later Han official Pan Piao think of the Northern Huns' (i.e., Northern Hsiung-nus') request to come to China and do "audience duty" (i.e., offer tribute)?

2. What was the nature and content of Pan Piao's reply sent to the Northern Huns?

3. Why did the Han decide to give double rations to those captured by the Southern Huns?

4. What was the advantage for Han China in the fact that the "Northern free-booters" (Northern Huns) were not yet unified with the Southern Huns?

5. In Liang Shang's letter, what were the strategic weak points and strong points of China in its confrontations with the barbarians?

IV.

The Huns

Everyone has heard of the Huns and Attila the Hun (c. A.D. 406–453), their brutal and able leader. The Huns, of uncertain Asiatic origin, arrived in Eastern Europe around A.D. 375 and then moved further westward, defeating the mighty Goths and Alans in the process. By A.D. 400 they had reached the borders of the Eastern Roman Empire, and by 432 they were intimidating the Romans into paying them tribute. In 451, Attila attacked the Western Empire and also moved against Gaul (France), which he failed to secure. He then briefly raided Italy, striking terror in the hearts of the citizens of Rome. His death in 453 quickly led to the complete disintegration of his empire.

A controversial theory identifies the Huns with the Hsiung-nu known to the Chinese; on this, see Section III above on the Hsiung-nu.

A. Ammianus Marcellinus

Ammianus Marcellinus (c. 330–395), the last great historian of the Roman Empire, was born to Greek parents in Antioch. Only the last eighteen books of his original 31-book history of the Roman Empire have survived to the present, and these cover the years of his own lifetime from 353 to 378 in considerable detail. His work culminates with extensive coverage of the Gothic invasion of Hadrianople in 978, the occasion of the death of the Roman emperor Valens. Marcellinus was not overtly anti-Christian but did reserve some satirical scorn for the failure of some of the religion's prominent professors to live up to its "pure and simple" aspects.

The scope of Marcellinus's coverage is wide, and for this he was admired by the great British historian of the Roman Empire, Edward Gibbon (1737–1794). His ethnographic descriptions of several peoples, Greek and non-Greek alike, are especially valuable to historians. His classic account of the Huns is the single most extensive contemporary description of these ferocious nomadic warriors by any historian.

The Nature of the Huns and Alans

Ammianus Marcellinus

The seed-bed and origin of all this destruction and of the various calamities inflicted by the wrath of Mars, which raged everywhere with unusual fury, I find to be this. The people of the Huns, who are mentioned only cursorily in ancient writers and who dwell beyond the Sea of Azov (Palus Maeotis) near the frozen ocean, are quite abnormally savage. From the moment of birth they make deep gashes in their children's cheeks, so that when in due course hair appears its growth is checked by the wrinkled scars; as they grow older this gives them the unlovely appearance of beardless eunuchs. They have squat bodies, strong limbs, and thick necks, and are so prodigiously ugly and bent that they might be two-legged animals, or the figures crudely carved from stumps which are seen on the parapets of bridges. Still, their shape, however disagreeable, is human; but their way of life is so rough that they have no use for fire or seasoned food, but live on the roots of wild plants and the half-raw flesh of any sort of animal, which they warm a little by placing it between their thighs and the backs of their horses. They have no buildings to shelter them, but avoid anything of the kind as carefully as we avoid living in the neighbourhood of tombs; not so much as a hut thatched with reeds is to be found among them. They roam at large over mountains and forests, and are inured from the cradle to cold, hunger, and thirst. On foreign soil only extreme necessity can persuade them to come under a roof, since they believe that it is not safe for them to do so. They wear garments of linen or of the skins of field-mice stitched together, and there is no difference between their clothing whether they are at home or abroad. Once they have put their necks into some dingy shirt they never take it off or change it till it rots and falls to pieces from incessant wear. They have round caps of fur on their heads, and protect their hairy legs with goatskins. Their shapeless shoes are not made on a last and make it hard to walk easily. In consequence they are ill-fitted to fight on foot, and remain glued to their horses, hardy but ugly beasts, on which they sometimes sit like women to perform their everyday business. Buying or selling, eating or drinking, are all done by day or night on horseback, and they even bow forward over their beasts' narrow necks to enjoy a deep and dreamy sleep. When they need to debate some important matter they conduct their conference in the same posture. They are not subject to the authority of any king, but break through any obstacle in their path under the improvised command of their chief men.

They sometimes fight *by challenging their foes to single combat*, but when they join battle they advance in packs, uttering their various warcries. Being lightly equipped and very sudden in their movements they can deliberately scatter and gallop about at random, inflicting tremendous slaughter; their extreme nimbleness enables them to force a rampart or pillage an enemy's camp before one catches sight of them. What makes them the most formidable of all warriors is that they shoot from a distance arrows tipped with sharp splinters of bone instead of the usual heads; these are joined to the shafts with wonderful skill. At close quarters they fight without regard for their lives, and while their opponents are guarding against sword-thrusts they catch their limbs in lassos of twisted cloth which make it impossible for them to ride or walk. None of them ploughs or ever touches a plough-handle. They have no fixed abode, no home or law or settled manner of life, but wander like refugees with the wagons in which they live. In these their wives weave their filthy clothing, mate with their husbands, give birth to their children, and rear them to the age of puberty. No one if asked can tell where he comes from, having been conceived in one place, born somewhere else, and reared even further off. You cannot make a truce with them, because they are quite unreliable and easily swayed by any breath of rumour which promises advantage; like unreasoning beasts they are entirely at the mercy of the maddest impulses. They are totally ignorant of the distinction between right and wrong, their speech is shifty and obscure, and they are under no restraint from religion or superstition. Their greed for gold is prodigious, and they are so fickle and prone to anger that often in a single day they will quarrel with their allies without any provocation, and then make it up again without anyone attempting to reconcile them.

This wild race, moving without encumbrances and consumed by a savage passion to pillage the property of others, advanced robbing and slaughtering over the lands of their neighbours till they reached the Alans. The Alans are the ancient Massagetae, and at this point it is relevant to discuss their origin and situation. This is a problem that has perplexed geographers, who have, however, *after much discussion found a reliable solution.*

The Danube, swollen by the waters of a number of tributaries, flows past the territory of the Sarmatians, which extends as far as the river Don (Tanais), the boundary between Europe and Asia. Beyond this the Alans inhabit the immense deserts of Scythia, deriving their name from the mountains. By repeated victories they gradually wore down the people next to them, and, like the Persians, incorporated them into a single nation bearing their own name. Of these the Nervi occupy the interior of the country near high peaks whose steep sides are frozen hard and swept by north winds. Next to them are the savage tribes of the Vidini and Geloni, who flay the skin from their dead enemies and make coverings of it for themselves and their chargers. On the borders of the Geloni are the Agathyrsi, who tattoo their bodies and colour their hair with a blue dye; the common people display only small spots widely spaced, but in the nobles they are larger and closer together. Beyond them, we are told, roam the Melanchlaenae and Anthropophagi, who live on human flesh. On account of this abominable habit all their neighbours have given them a wide berth and removed to distant regions. In consequence the entire north-eastern tract as far as China has remained uninhabited. In another direction, near the country of the Amazons, the Alans approach the East and form populous and widespread communities. These stretch into Asia, and I have been told that they reach as far as the Ganges, the river which intersects India and empties into the southern sea.

Thus the Alans, whose various tribes there is no point in enumerating, extend over both parts of the earth *(Europe and Asia)*. But, although they are widely separated and wander in their nomadic way over immense areas, they have in course of time come to be known by one name and are all compendiously called Alans, because their character, their wild way of life, and their weapons are the same everywhere. They have no huts and make no use of the plough, but live upon meat and plenty of milk. They use wagons covered with a curved canopy of bark, and move in these over the endless desert. When they come to a grassy place they arrange their carts in a circle and feed like wild animals; then, having exhausted the forage available, they again settle what one might call their mobile towns upon their vehicles, and move on. In these wagons the males couple with the women and their children are born and reared; in fact, these wagons are their permanent dwellings and, wherever they go, they look upon them as their ancestral home.

They drive their cattle before them and pasture them with their flocks, and they pay particular attention to the breeding of horses. The plains there are always green and there are occasional patches of fruit-trees, so that, wherever they go, they never lack food and fodder. This is because the soil is damp and there are numerous rivers. Those whose age or sex makes them unfit to fight stay by the wagons and occupy themselves in light work, but the younger men, who are inured to riding from earliest boyhood, think it beneath their dignity to walk and are all trained in a variety of ways to be skilful warriors. This is why the Persians too, who are of Scythian origin, are such expert fighters.

Almost all Alans are tall and handsome, with yellowish hair and frighteningly fierce eyes. They are active and nimble in the use of arms and in every way a match for the Huns, but less savage in their habits and way of life. Their raiding and hunting expeditions take them as far as the Sea of Azov and the Crimea, and also to Armenia and Media. They take as much delight in the dangers of war as quiet and peaceful folk in ease and leisure. They regard it as the height of good fortune to lose one's life in battle; those who grow old and die a natural death are bitterly reviled as degenerate cowards. Their proudest boast is to have killed a man, no matter whom, and their most coveted trophy is to use the flayed skins of their decapitated foes as trappings for their horses.

No temple or shrine is to be found among them, not so much as a hut thatched with straw, but their savage custom is to stick a naked sword in the earth and worship it as the god of war, the presiding deity of the regions over which they range. They have a wonderful way of foretelling the future. They collect straight twigs of osier, and at an appointed time sort them out uttering a magic formula, and in this way they obtain clear knowledge of what is to come. They are all free from birth, and slavery is unknown among them. To this day they choose as their leaders men who have proved their worth by long experience in war. Now I must return to what remains of my main theme.

The Huns and Alans Expel the Goths from Their Homes

The Huns, overrunning the territory of those Alans who border on the Greuthungi and are commonly called the Don Alans, killed and stripped many of them, and made a pact of friendship with the survivors. This success emboldened them to make a sudden inroad on the rich and extensive realm of Ermenrich, a warlike king whose many heroic exploits had made him a terror to his neighbours. Ermenrich was hard hit by the violence of this unexpected storm. For some time he endeavoured to stand his ground, but exaggerated reports circulated of the dreadful fate which awaited him, and he found release from his fears by taking his own life. He was succeeded as king by Vithimir, who resisted the Alans for a time, relying on the help of other Huns whom he had hired to support him. But after many defeats he was overwhelmed by superior force and lost his life in battle. The guardianship of his young son Videric was undertaken by Alatheus and Saphrax, experienced commanders of proved courage, but their plans were frustrated by circumstances, and they had to abandon any hope of successful resistance. So they prudently withdrew to the line of the river Dniester (Danastius), which waters the wide plains between the Danube and the Dnieper (Borysthenes).

Athanaric the chief of the Thervingi, against whom, as I have already said, Valens had recently taken the field to punish him for sending help to Procopius, heard of these unexpected events and attempted to maintain his ground, being resolved to put forth all his strength if he should be attacked like the rest. Accordingly he took up his position in a good spot near the banks of the Dniester but some distance from the defensive works of the Greuthungi, and sent Munderic, who later commanded on the Arabian frontier, together with Lagariman and some other notables twenty miles ahead to watch for the approach of the enemy, while he himself marshalled his army undisturbed. But things turned out very differently from what he expected. The Huns, who are good guessers, suspected that there was a larger force further off. So they paid no attention to the troops they had seen, who had lain down to rest as if they had no enemy near them. Then the Huns forded the river by moonlight, and took what was undoubtedly the best course. They forestalled the possibility of any warning reaching the enemy by making a rapid assault on Athanaric himself, and before he could recover from the surprise of their first onset drove him with some losses on their own part to take refuge in rugged mountain country. This new situation and the fear that there was worse to follow constrained him to erect a high rampart extending from the Pruth (Gerasus) to the Danube and skirting the territory of the Taifali. He believed that this hastily but carefully constructed barrier would ensure his security. But while he was pushing on this important work he was hard pressed by the rapid advance of the Huns, who have overwhelmed him if the weight of booty they were carrying had not forced them to desist.

A report, however, now spread widely among the other Gothic tribes that a hitherto unknown race of men had appeared from some remote corner of the earth, uprooting and destroying everything in its path like a whirlwind descending from high mountains. Weakened by the lack of the necessities of life the greater part of the people abandoned Athanaric, and looked for a dwelling far from all knowledge of the barbarians. After much debate where to settle they fixed upon Thrace as the most eligible refuge for two reasons, first, because of its fertility, and second, because it is separated by the broad stream of the Danube from the regions exposed to the thunderbolts of the alien Mars. This decisions met with unanimous support.

Study Questions

1. What, by Marcellinus, made the Huns so fearful?

2. What were some of the things the Huns did on horseback?

3. What were some of the Huns' battle tactics?

4. What, by Marcellinus, made the Huns "the most formidable of all warriors"?

5. How does Marcellinus describe some of the characteristics of the Huns?

6. Who were the Alans, and were they pastoral nomads like the Huns?

7. What did the Alans worship as the god of war?

8. After the Huns defeated the Alans and secured a pact with the survivors among them, what people did their combined forces move against next?

B. Isidore de Seville

I sidore (Isidorus Hispalensis, c. 560–636), bishop of Seville, was
born to a prominent Roman family in Visigothic Spain. A doctor
of the Church, he was widely regarded as the most learned man
of his time. He wrote extensively on theological, historical, and even
linguistic topics. His best-known work, the vast encyclopaedia
Etymologiae, was incomplete at the time of his death but included
sections on language, geography, law, medicine, and theology. It was
widely consulted during the Middle Ages. Among his minor works is
his *History of the Goths, Vandals, and Suevi,* from which the passage
below is excerpted. In it he attempts to impose some theological
meaning on the depredations of the Huns. Would you agree with his
perspectives?

History of the Goths, Vandals, and Suevi

Isidore de Sevelle

Aetius was then removed from military authority by order of the Emperor Valentinian, and when Theudered attacked the city of Narbonne with a long siege and with famine, he was again put to flight by Litorius, the leader of the Roman soldiers, with the help of the Huns. But Litorius, after first being successful against the Goths, inconsiderately went to war with them a second time, deceived by the signs of demons and the responses of soothsayers. The Roman army was lost and he perished after being pitiably defeated, and caused it to be realized of how much avail that multitude which died with him could have been if he had chosen to make use of faith rather than the treacherous portents of demons.

Then Theudered, after concluding peace with the Romans, again fought against the Huns who were laying waste the provinces of Gaul with savage pillaging and destroying very many cities; he fought against them in open battle on the plains of Châlons with the help of the Roman general Aetius, and there he died in the course of the battle while he was winning. But the Goths, under the leadership of Thurismund, the son of King Theudered, fought so bravely that between the first battle and the last about three hundred thousand men were laid low.

At the same time many signs appeared in heaven and on earth, by whose portents such a cruel war might be indicated. Continuous earthquakes occurred, and in the East the moon was darkened. In the West a comet appeared and shone for some time with a huge size. In the North the sky became reddish like fire or blood, and mixed with the fiery redness there were brighter lines in the form of reddish spears. Nor was it astonishing that in the case of such a large mass of slaughtered men such a manifold demonstration of signs should be shown by God.

The Huns indeed, after having been slaughtered almost to the point of extermination, left Gaul with their king Attila and fled to Italy, breaking into several cities. There some died of hunger and others after being struck by heaven-sent plagues. When, moreover, an army was sent by the Emperor Marcianus, they were cut down by a violent plague, and having suffered greatly from it, returned to their own lands; and soon after their king Atilla returned, he died.

Immediately great struggles for the possession of the kingdom began among his sons. And so the Huns, who had previously suffered losses by so many disasters, again slaughtered each other with their own weapons. With regard to them it is astonishing that whereas every battle entails a loss for nations, this people, on the other hand, should be of service by dying: but this is so because they are used to discipline the faithful, just like the people of the Persian nation.

For they are the scourge of God's fury, and as often as his indignation goes forth against the faithful, the latter are scourged by them in order that, corrected by their blows, they may restrain themselves from worldly desires and from sin and possess the inheritance of the kingdom of heaven. But this nation is so savage that when they suffer hunger during war they open the veins of horses and so remove their hunger by drinking blood.

In the era 490 (452), the first year of Marcianus' rule, Thurismund, the son of Theudered, was raised to the kingship, which he held for a year. Since at the very beginning of his reign he was cruel and harmful and excited hostility and did many things with great arrogance, he was killed by his brothers Theuderic and Frigdaric.

Study Questions

1. What, according to Isidore, happened to the Huns immediately after Attila's death?

2. What, according to Isidore's theory, was the use to which God put the Huns?

C. Jordanes

Jordanes, a historian of Gothic descent and likely a monk in Constantinople, flourished ca. A.D. 550. Two of his works have survived: the *Romana*, a summary or outline of Roman history, and the so-called *Getica*, his account of Gothic history.

Jordanes obviously holds some animosity towards the Huns, the conquerors of his own people. He is well known for his superstitious speculation on the ancestry of the Huns. This passage from his *Getica* reproduced here is another fragment of information on the Huns available to historians.

The Gothic History of Jordanes

Charles Christopher Mierow, Ph.D.

But after a short space of time, as Orosius relates, the race of the Huns, fiercer than ferocity itself, flamed forth against the Goths. We learned from old traditions that their origin was as follows: Filimer, king of the Goths, son of Gadaric the Great, who was the fifth in succession to hold the rule of the Getae after their departure from the island of Scandza—and who, as we have said, entered the land of Scythia with his tribe—found among his people certain witches, whom he called in his native tongue *Haliurunnae*. Suspecting these women, he expelled them from the midst of his race and compelled them to wander in solitary exile afar from his army. There the unclean spirits, who beheld them as they wandered through the wilderness, bestowed their embraces upon them and begat this savage race, which dwelt at first in the swamps, a stunted, foul and puny tribe, scarcely human and having no language save one which bore but slight resemblance to human speech. Such was the descent of the Huns who came to the country of the Goths.

This cruel tribe, as Priscus the historian relates, settled on the farther bank of the Maeotic swamp. They were fond of hunting and had no skill in any other art. After they had grown to a nation, they disturbed the peace of neighboring races by theft and rapine. At one time, while hunters of their tribe were as usual seeking for game on the farthest edge of Maeotis, they saw a doe unexpectedly appear to their sight and enter the swamp, acting as a guide of the way; now advancing and again standing still. The hunters followed and crossed on foot the Maeotic swamp, which they had supposed was impassable as the sea. Presently the unknown land of Scythia disclosed itself and the doe disappeared. Now in my opinion the evil spirits, from whom the Huns are descended, did this from envy of the Scythians. And the Huns, who had been wholly ignorant that there was another world beyond Maeotis, were now filled with admiration for the Scythian land. As they were quick of mind, they believed that this path, utterly unknown to any age of the past, had been divinely revealed to them. They returned to their tribe, told them what had happened, praised Scythia and persuaded the people to hasten thither along the way they had found by the guidance of the doe. As many as they captured, when they thus entered Scythia for the first time, they sacrificed to Victory. The remainder they conquered and made subject to themselves. Like a whirlwind of nations they swept across the great swamp and at once fell upon the Alpidzuri, Alcildzuri, Itimari, Tuncarsi and Boisci, who bordered on that part of Scythia. The Alani also, who were their equals in battle, but unlike them in civilization, manners and appearance, they exhausted by their incessant attacks and subdued. For by the terror of their features they inspired great fear in those whom perhaps they did not really surpass in war. They made their foes flee in horror because their swarthy aspect was fearful, and they had, if I may call it so, a sort of shapeless lump, not a head, with pin-holes rather than eyes. Their hardihood is evident in their wild appearance, and they are beings who are cruel to their children on the very day they are born. For they cut the cheeks of the males with a sword, so that before they receive the nourishment of milk they must learn to endure wounds. Hence they grow old beardless and their young men are without comeliness, because a face furrowed by the sword spoils, by its scars, the natural beauty of a beard. They are short in stature, quick in bodily movement, alert horsemen, broad shouldered, ready in the use of bow and arrow, and have firm-set necks which are ever erect in pride. Though they live in the form of men, they have the cruelty of wild beasts.

When the Getae beheld this active race that had invaded many nations, they took fright and consulted with their king how they might escape from such a foe. Now although Hermanaric, king of the Goths, was the conqueror of many tribes, as we have said above, yet while he was deliberating on this invasion of the Huns, the treacherous tribe of Rosomoni, who at that time were among those who owed him their homage, took this chance to catch him unawares. For when the king had given orders that a certain woman of the tribe I have mentioned, Sunilda by name, should be bound to wild horses and torn apart by driving them at full speed in opposite directions (for he was roused to fury by her husband's treachery to him), her brothers Sarus and Ammius came to avenge their sister's death and plunged a sword into Hermanaric's side. Enfeebled by this blow, he dragged out a miserable existence in bodily weakness. Balamber, king of the Huns, took advantage of his ill health to move an army into the country of the Ostrogoths, from whom the Visigoths had already separated because of some dispute. Meanwhile Hermanaric, who was unable to endure either the pain of his wound or the inroads of the Huns, died full of days at the great age of one hundred and ten years. The fact of his death enabled the Huns to prevail over those Goths who, as we have said, dwelt in the east and were called Ostrogoths.

Study Questions

1. What, according to Jordanes, was the ancestry of the Huns?

2. According to Jordanes, how did the Huns treat their children? Why?

3. What, according to Jordanes, enabled the Huns to prevail over the Ostrogoths?

V.

The Turks

Europeans and North Americans are sometimes surprised to learn that the Turks were known to China and were at least as aggressive towards the Chinese in the sixth and seventh centuries as they were hundreds of years later towards Islamic and European civilizations. But over the last century, careful scholarly investigation has shown that the earliest known homeland of the Turkic peoples was what we now call Mongolia. Known to the Chinese as *T'u-chueh*, the Turks founded a great steppe empire in the sixth century and periodically menaced T'ang dynasty China until the eighth century.

Turkic peoples today live over an extended area, from Turkey in the west to the former Soviet republics and the so-called "autonomous region" of Xinjiang (Chinese Turkestan) in the People's Republic of China. The most important identifying characteristics of the Turkic peoples are their language, history, and religion (Islam); the modern concept of "race" is irrelevant to the Turkic identity because Turkic peoples display various racial or phenotypical characteristics. Many Turks in China and the Central Asian republics of the former Soviet Union are Asiatic in appearance, while many Turks in Turkey today resemble Western Europeans.

A. Chou shu

T he *Chou shu* ("Chou History") records the history of the
medieval Chou dynasty (A.D. 557–577), a short-lived regime in
northern China. Itself a remnant of the Turkic T'o-pa
(Tobgatch) dynasty (A.D. 386–535), the Chou rulers were in a
precarious situation vis-a-vis the newly ascendant T'u-chueh Turks.
The *Chou shu* was compiled from Chou materials several decades
after the downfall of the dynasty and the unification of all China
under the Sui (A.D. 581–618) and T'ang (A.D. 618–907) dynasties. It
contains some of the earliest Chinese accounts of the Turks.

The Early Turks
From the *Chou Shu*

The 'Turks' were in fact a separate kind of Hiung-nu, with the family surname A-shï-no, who became a distinct horde and were afterwards crushed by neighbouring States, which utterly annihilated the clan. There was a lad just upon ten years of age: the soldier men, observing his smallness, had not the heart to kill him, so they cut off his feet and pitched him into the jungly morass, where a she-wolf fed him flesh; and when he grew up he had connection with the wolf, who in consequence became *enceinte*. The king of those parts, hearing this lad was still in existence, repeatedly sent to kill him. The messenger, seeing the wolf at his side, was about to kill the wolf too, on which the wolf fled to the northern mountains of Kao-ch'ang state. The mountains contained a recess, and in this recess there was a fertile plain several hundred *li* in circuit, with mountains on all four sides. The wolf hid away in it, and then gave birth to ten sons. The ten sons growing up got elsewhere wives who became pregnant, and after that they each had a family name, of which A-shï-no was one.

Their descendants increased in numbers until they gradually reached some hundred households, and after living in company for several generations they left the recess and became vassals of the Ju-ju, occupying parts south of the Gold Mountains and doing iron work for the Ju-ju. One or some of the Gold Mountains were shaped like a helmet, and their way of calling a helmet was *t'uh-küeh*, in consequence of which they took this as an appellation.

Another account has it that the forebears of the Turks emanated from Soh state, north of the Hiung-nu. The chief men were called A-pang-pu, of whom there were seventeen brethren, one of whom was called I-chih Ni-shï-tu, born of a wolf. Pang-pu and the others were all of a foolish disposition, so that the state got annihilated. Ni-shï-tu being separated from the rest got imbued with a weird influence, and was able to summon the wind and rain. He married two wives, said to be the daughters of the Genius of Summer and the Genius of Winter. One became *enciente* and gave birth to four sons, and one was changed into a white swan. The one's country was between the River A-fu and River Kien and was styled K'i-kuh: another had his country at the Ch'u-chêh River. One of them occupied the Tsien-az Ch'u-chêh-shï Mountains: this was the eldest son. On the mountains there were still some of the A-pang-pu progeny, most of whom were suffering from cold and exposure. The eldest son produced fire for them and nourished them with warmth, so that they all got safely out of their predicament, and then joined in honouring the eldest son as lord, with the appellation of Turk, that is the tribe of Noh-tu-luh.

No-tu-luh had ten wives, and the children they bore all took their mother's clan for family name, and A-shï-no was the child of his youngest wife. When No-tu-luh died, it was desired to elect one from among the children of the ten mothers, so they proceeded in company to a spot beneath a great tree and formed the following agreement: Whoever shall jump the highest up towards the tree shall be proclaimed chosen. A-shï-no's son, though young, being the one who jumped highest, was acclaimed as lord under the style A-hien tribe.

Though the above accounts differ yet they agree so far as wolf's progeny goes.

After that, it goes on to say, T'u-mên's horde grew strong and they first appeared on our frontiers to buy silks and floss, expressing a desire to open relations with China.

In the 11th year of Ta-t'ung, T'ai-tsu sent a Tsiu-ts'üan Tartar An-noh-p'an-t'o on a mission to them. In their state they all congratulated themselves, saying: Now that a great country's envoy has come, our country will flourish. In the 12th year T'u-mên accordingly despatched an envoy to submit local articles.

At that time the T'ieh-lêh were on the point of attacking the Ju-ju; T'u-mên led those under his command to intercept them and routed them, on which he forced to surrender the whole body to the number of 50,000 tents, and taking advantage of this accession of strength proceeded to demand a marriage-alliance with the Ju-ju. The Ju-ju lord A-na-kwei was greatly enraged and sent men to revile him saying: You are our forge slaves! How dare you give forth this language? T'u-mên was also enraged, killed their envoys, and thus broke with them, seeking a marriage alliance with us instead. T'ai-tsu consented to it, and in the 6th moon of the 7th year gave him as wife the Princess Ch'ang-loh of Wei. This year the Emperor Wên Ti of Wei died, and T'u-mên sent a mission of condolence, and received a parting gift of 200 horses.

In the 1st moon of the 1st year of the Wei Emperor Fei Ti, T'u-mên took out a force to attack the Ju-ju, and completely routed them to the north of Hwai-hwang. A-na-kwei committed suicide. His son, An-lo-ch'ên fled to Ts'i. The rest of his multitude set up as lord in his place. A-na-kwei's uncle, 'Uncle Têng,' and T'u-mên then styled himself the Ili Khan as though the ancient Shen-yü. He styled his wife Khatun, as though the ancient Yen-chï.

When T'u-mên died, his son K'o-lo succeeded. K'o-lo's title was Yih-sih-ki Khan, and he again defeated Têng Shuh-tsz in the Muh-lai Mountains to the northward of Woh-ye.

In the 3rd moon of the second year, K'o-lo sent envoys to submit 50,000 horses. When K'o-lo died, his younger brother Sz-kin succeeded with the title of Muh-han Khan; another of Sz-kin's names was Yen-tu. His aspect had remarkable features. His face was over a foot broad, with a very ruddy tint, and his eyes were of greenish hue. His disposition was hard and tyrannical, bent upon feats of war. Accordingly he led troops to attack Têng-shuh-tsz whom he annihilated. Shuh-tsz with his shattered remnants came to take refuge.

Sz-kin (i.e., the djigin) furthermore broke up the Ts'oh-t'ah to the west, drove away the Kitans to the east, annexed the K'i-kuh to the north, and overawed the various countries beyond our frontiers. His land extended from the west of the Liao Sea westwards to the West Sea, 10,000 li from east to west, and from the Desert northwards to the North Sea, 6,000 li from north to south, all which was under him.

Their custom was to let their hair cover them and have the lapel to the left. They live in felt tents, moving from place to place accordingly as they find water and grass. Pasturing their flocks, and hunting with the bow is their occupation. They despise the old and esteem the robust. They have little sense of decency, and none of courtesy or right, just like the ancient Hiung-nu.

When the accession of a new lord took place, the more important ministers attached to the court carried him in a piece of felt, turning round after the sun nine times, and each time all his subjects made obeisance to him. When the obeisances were over he was helped up on horseback and a cloth was twisted round his throat until he was all but put an end to, after which it was loosened and he was hurriedly, asked: How many years' Khan can you act as? Their lord being in a perturbed state of mind was unable to decide carefully how many, and his subjects used to take what he said as a criterion of the length or brevity in number.

Their high officers include the *jabghu*, next the *moh*, next the *t'êh-lêh*, next the *sz-li-fah*, next the *t'u-t'un-fah*, and a number of other smaller officials, of whom there are 28 ranks in all, the whole of them hereditary.

Amongst their arms are the bow, arrow, buzzing arrow, cuirass, spear, sword, cutlass; and carried at the belt they also have a *fuh-t'uh* ornament. On their standards they make use of a gold wolf's head. Their soldiers of the guard are called *fu-li*, which in the *Hia* language also means 'wolf,' for they were originally derived from a wolf, and they were minded not to forget antiquity.

In raising armies or levying taxes upon the miscellaneous flocks, they always carve in wood to denote numbers and have besides a golden barbed arrow which they impress as a seal upon wax as an evidentiary sign.

Their penal laws visit with death all such offences as rebellion, murder, adultery with married women, and stealing tethered horses. Fornication with unmarried women is punished with a heavy fine, and the girl is married to the offender. Injury done in quarrel is met with an amercement of substance according to its gravity. Stealing horses and other objects is visited by a mulct of ten or more times [the quantity or value].

The bodies of deceased persons are laid out in the tent, and the descendants and various relatives and dependants of both sexes each kill a sheep or horse, which they set out in front of the tent by way of oblation. They go round the tent trotting their horses seven times, and, proceeding in a body to the door of the tent, gash their faces with knives and weep, tears and blood coursing down together: this is repeated seven times, when they stop. They select a day, and take the horses which the deceased used to ride, and clothes which he wore, etc., and burn them together with the corpse, collecting the remaining ashes for sepulture on suitable opportunity. Those who die in the spring and summer are kept until the vegetation begins to wilt. Those who die in the autumn and winter are kept until the luxuriant foliage is in full bloom. They then dig a pit and bury them. On the day of burial the relations and dependants set up oblation, trot their horses, and gash their faces, as before with the death ceremonies. When the sepulture is finished, they erect stones and set up marks, the number of stones being in proportion to the human lives taken by the deceased during his career. Moreover they stick up on the mark all the heads of the sheep and horses sacrificed. On this day males and females all dress themselves up in their best, and assemble at the place of burial, and any men who fall in love with the girls there on their return home at once send persons with marriage proposals, to which the parents as a rule do not object. When fathers or paternal uncles die the sons, younger brothers, or nephews marry their stepmothers, aunts by marriage, and sisters-in-law; but no man in a higher generation can have incestuous relation with those in a lower degree.

Though they move from place to place indefinitely, still they each have their share of land. The Khan always had his *habitat* in the Tu-kin Mountains. His tent opened to the East, as a mark of respect to the place where the Sun rises. Every year at the head of his nobles he made sacrifice to his ancestors' vault, and moreover during the middle decade of the 5th moon he assembled other people, and did water obeisance in worship of the Spirit of Heaven.

West of Tu-kin 500 *li* there is a high mountain which stands prominently out, and upon which there is no vegetation: it is called *Puh têng-nying li* or in the Hia language 'Spirit of Earth.'

Their written characters resemble those of the *Hu*; but they have no knowledge of annual calendars, and simply keep note by the blooming grass.

When Sz-kin's horde had become considerable, he sent envoys to apply for the execution of Têng Shuh-tsz and his friends. T'sai-tsu consented, and gathered together Shuh-tsz and those under him to the number of 3,000 men, handing them over to the envoy, who butchered them outside the Green Gate.

The third year Sz-kin attacked the T'u-kuh-hun and routed them. In the 2nd year of Ming Ti, Sz-kin sent envoys to come and submit local articles. In the 1st year of Pao-ting he again on three occasions sent envoys to bring tribute of his local objects. At that time we were struggling with Ts'i, and war chariots were annually on the move; hence alliances were more than once made with him, so as to have him as an external reinforcement. Now during the time of Kung Ti of Wei Sz-kin had promised to send in a daughter for T'ai-tsu, who however died before the agreement was fixed. After that Sz-kin promised another daughter to Kao-tsu; and before the betrothal was complete the Ts'i men also sent to beg for a marriage. Sz-kin, greedy of the richer presents, was on the point of breaking off, and on this under a decree of Yang Tsien, prefect-governor of Liang Chou, with K'ing, Price of Wupêh, went to complete the negotiations. When K'ing and his companions arrived they gave him a lecture on the duty of keeping word, on which Sz-kin broke off with the Ts'i envoy and decided upon the nuptials, at the same time offering to march eastwards with all his powers, as is related in the chapter devoted to Yang Tsien.

In the third year a decree ordered Yang Chung, Duke of Sui, to lead a host of 10,000 and join the Turks in attacking Ts'i. Chung's army having crossed the Hing Range, Sz-kin at the head of 100,000 horsemen effected a junction with him. In the 1st moon of the following year they unsuccessfully attacked the lord of Ts'i at Tsin-yang. Sz-kin then returned, after allowing his troops to plunder where they could. Chung spoke to Kao Tsu saying: 'The Turkish troopers are disgusted with the meagreness of their rewards and promotion: their commanding officers are numerous, but there is no discipline: why suppose it difficult to keep them in hand? It is all owing to the recent yarns of envoys, making out that they are so powerful, with the object of making government magnify their missions, out of which they derive solid advantage for the journey undertaken. The Court accepts their vain tales, and officers and men shudder at imaginary dangers; but the freebooters' aspect is only make-believe solid, though as a matter of fact they are easy enough to tackle. Now, my view is this. All the envoys from first to last may be decapitated.' Kao Tsu did not accept this advice, and this year Sz-kin once more sent envoys to bring offerings, and furthermore suggested a campaign eastwards. A decree ordered Yang Chung to lead out an army beyond Woh-ye, and Hu, Duke of Tsin, to hasten to Loh-yang to support him, but when Hu was defeated in battle Sz-kin retired. In the 5th year a decree ordered Shun, Duke of Ch'ên; the Minister of State Yü-wên Kwei; Tou I, Duke of Shên-wu; and Yang Tsien, Duke of Nan-an to go and fetch the bride. In the 2nd year of T'ien-ho Sz-kin again sent a mission with offerings. When Shun, Duke of Ch'ên, and his companions arrived, Sz-kin once more proved faithless to Ts'i; and just then there was a portentous thunderstorm, so he consented. Shun and his companions brought her back as Empress. In the 4th year Sz-kin again sent a mission to offer some horses. When Sz-kin died, his younger brother, T'a-pol Khan assumed the succession.

Ever since Sz-kin's time their state had grown in wealth and power and had been bent upon terrorising China. The Court, having made a marriage alliance with them, supplied them annually with silks, floss, and gay embroideries to the extent of 100,000 pieces; and those Turks who were at the metropolis were moreover entertained in the most hospitable way, there being often whole thousands of them clad in rich garments and feasting on flesh. The Ts'i-men, dreading their plundering raids, also emptied the treasuries for their benefit. T'a-poh became in consequence even more presumptuous, and when there were arrivals he appeared at the head of his creatures saying: So long as my two sons in the South are dutiful, what need is there for us to fear we shall have no good things?

In the 2nd year of Kien-têh T'a-poh sent a mission to offer some horses, and when Ts'i was extinguished, the Ts'i governor of Ting Chou, Kao, Shao-i, Prince of Fan-yang, fled from Ma Yih to him. T'a-poh recognized Shao-i as Emperor of Ts'i and, rallying the latter's forces, gave out that he was going to avenge him. In the 4th moon of the 1st year of Süan-chêng accordingly T'a-poh made a raid upon Yu Chou, massacring and plundering the inhabitants. The dignitary Liu Hiung led a force to repel the enemy, but was defeated after desperate fighting. Kao Tsu then personally took general command of the imperial armies, and was just on the point of marching northwards when his Majesty died, and the army was marched back. This winter T'a-poh again raided the frontier, surrounded Ta'iu-ti'üan, and retired after a general plunder. In the 1st year of Ta-siang T'a-poh made another application for a marriage alliance, and the Emperor conferred a patent upon the daughter of Chao, Prince of Chao, as Princess of Ts'ien-kin, to be his wife: he also sent persons to take into their custody Shao-i and bring him to the frontier. But T'a-poh would not obey the mandate and went on raiding Ping Chou. It was only in the 2nd year of Ta-siang that he sent a mission to offer presents; also to fetch the princess: but he still declined to deliver up Shao-i. The Emperor then ordered Ho-Jo-i to go and expostulate, when at last he gave up Shao-i. So it runs.

[This is the end of the *Chou Shu* account, which is the oldest: that is to say, though compiled about the same time as the *Peh Shï* and *Sui Shu*, it is compiled from records which are older than the records used for compiling the other two. There is no earlier mention of the Turks. The *Wei Shu* brings down the Juan-juan and Toba Wei history to A.D. 532, mentioning even a Hiung-nu family of Yü-wên speaking a different dialect from the Sein-pi: but not a word is said of the Turks, whose concrete existence may be said to begin (between 533 and 552) with Tumêu's father Notoru].

Study Questions

1. What is common to the two accounts of the origins of the Turks here?
2. When the Turk leader T'u-men proposed marriage-alliance with the Ju-ju (also known as the Jou-jan or Juan-juan), what was the response?
3. What did T'u-men do in response to their response?
4. What descriptions of the Turks' way of life are given here?

5. What was the law of the Turks like? How were offenses such as rebellion, murder, and adultery with a married woman punished?

6. What were some of the Turkic funerary customs?

7. What did the Chou dynasty in China send to the Turks?

8. The Chou and Ch'i dynasties in China both gave wealth to the Turks. What did the Turk leader T'a-poh say about this?

B. Chiu T'ang shu

The *Chiu T'ang shu* ("Old T'ang History"), a work in 200 chapters, was completed in A.D. 954, four decades after the fall of the T'ang dynasty (A.D. 618–907). The passages excerpted below detail the policy deliberations at the court of T'ai-tsung (r. A.D. 626–649), the second and greatest of the T'ang emperors. T'ai-tsung was part Turk and spoke Turkish, so he well understood the workings and intricacies of the situation among the Turks. He dealt wisely with the Turks, who eventually submitted to him and recognized him as their "Heavenly Khan. " (T'ai-tsung, then, wore two hats: Emperor of the Chinese and Heavenly Khan of the Turks and other pastoral nomadic peoples.)

The Early Turks
From the *Chiu T'ang Shu*

Shih-poh-pi, the T'uh-li Khagan, was Shï-pih Khagan's best-born son, and Hieh-li's nephew. During the Sui period Ta-yeh, when T'uh-li was only a few years old, Shï-pih sent him to command the soldiers of his Eastern ordo, styled the Ni-pu *shad*, north of the Sui Princess of Hwai-nan, and then gave him [her] as wife. When Hieh-li succeeded to the throne [Shih-poh-pi] was made T'uh-li Khagan, his ordo lying north from Yu Chou. T'uh-li in the East [thus] had particular command over the score or more of Hi, Sih, and such tribes; but levying imposts immoderately as he did, most of those tribes felt aggrieved at him. At the beginning of Chêng-kwan the Hi, Sih, etc., came together to belong to China. Hieh-li, angry at his thus losing the horde, sent him north to march against the Yen-t'o, when he again lost an army, on which he was imprisoned and flogged.

Now T'uh-li ever since Wu-têh times had bound himself deeply to T'ai-tsung, and T'ai-tsung too had conciliated him through kind and just treatment, forming a brotherhood alliance with him before they separated. Afterwards when Hieh-li's administrations went wrong, sudden demands for troops were made upon T'uh-li, who refused to supply them, from which circumstance hostile feelings arose. In the 3rd year of Chêng-kwan he made a formal application to come to Court. His Majesty, addressing the attendant ministers, said:—'I noticed that the guiders of the state under former dynasties who have given anxious thought to the people's weal have enjoyed a long tenure of rule, whilst those who have made men subservient to their own personal gratification have inevitably come to dynastic grief. In the present case the reason why people of the northern *fan* have perished is undoubtedly because their prince has been unprincely, in such wise as to force upon T'uh-li the wish to come to Court. If he were not hard put to it, how could things come to this pass? That the barbarian Tartars should be weak means that the frontier marches are unalarmed, which is, of course, very satisfactory. Still, when we contemplate their anarchical conditions, we cannot but yet feel alarmed, and the reason why is that we grow anxious lest similar shortcomings of our own should develop into an analogous revolution. At this moment the horizon of my sight and the scope of my own hearing are limited in extent, and I can but therefore rely upon you, gentlemen, to give me your most loyal assistance and support; be you not remiss in your "opposition" duties.' Shortly after that T'uh-li was attacked by Hieh-li, and sent envoys to us to crave an army. T'ai tsung, addressing the ministers near him, said:—'I have allied myself in brotherhood with T'uh-li, and I cannot but proceed to his rescue.' Tu Ju-hwei advancing said:— 'The barbarian Tartars have no faith, as we know of old, and, though the Government keep treaty with them, they are sure to break it themselves. Much better take advantage of their confusion to capture them, or as the saying goes, "seize hold of their anarchy to crush them out of life."' T-ai-tsung agreed with this, and so ordered General Chou Fan to encamp at T'ai-yüan with a view advancing to the capture, whilst T'uh-li at the head of his horde came to take refuge with us. T'ai-tsung treated him with very great courtesy, and repeatedly gave him to eat from the Imperial table. In the 4th year he was appointed Right General of the Guards, and patented as second-class Prince of Peh-p'ing with manor allowances calculated at

700 households; and the host of soldiers under him were quartered in the Shun and Yu prefectures; and thus were conducted the tribes back to their *fan*. T'si-tsung, addressing him, said:—'In the past, when your grandfather K'i-min utterly lost his army, and as a solitary individual threw himself upon Sui, the Sui family assisted him up again, so that he became strong and powerful. Though recipient of Sui's kindness, he never made any requital. And when it came to your father Shï-pih, he even became a nuisance to the Sui family. Ever since your time not a year has passed but what you have invaded or harassed China. Heaven has of a truth chastised you with evil, and sent catastrophes down upon you. Your hordes are scattered in confusion, and have almost perished entirely. You now come to us in your extremity, and the reasons why we do not set you up as Khagan is just because of the former K'i-min affair. The old system shall be entirely changed with a view to China's lasting peace, and the enduring solidity of your agnatic clans. For this reason you are appointed a *tutuh*, and you will have to keep your tribes in order according to our country's system and you must not improperly invade or plunder each other. If there is any disobedience, you will incur severe punishment.' In the 5th year he was sent for to Court, but died of sickness on the road at Ping Chou, aged 29. T'ai-tsung set up a lament for him, and commanded the *shilang* Ts'ên Wên-pên to compose the inscription for him tombstone. His son Ho-lo-huh succeeded. T'uh-li's younger brother Kieh-shê-shwai had in the beginning of Chêng-kwan entered Court, and had since occupied the post of *chung-lang-tsiang*. In the 13th year, when following in the suite to the Kiu-ch'êng Palace, he secretly collected the assistance of over 40 men of the tribes, who rushed together in a body with Ho-lo-huh to make a night assault upon the Imperial camp. They succeeded in getting over the fourth canvas-barrier, drew their bows, and let fly promiscuously, killing a score or more of the guards. The subordinate officer Sun Wu-k'ai energetically fought them at the head of his men, on which they retired, and, flying north, crossed the River Wei with the intention of taking refuge with their tribesmen, but they were soon all caught and decapitated. A mandate excused Ho-lo-huh, who was transported beyond the Range.

As a result of Hieh-li's defeat some of his tribe settlements either fled to the Siehyen-t'o or to Turkestan, but a large number of them came to surrender. There was a mandate issued to discuss some means for pacifying the borders. Most of the officers at Court said that the Turks, presuming on their strength, had for a very long time harassed and disturbed China, but that now Heaven had truly undone them; that their coming over to us in their extremity was not in reality out of any longing for reform: to take advantage of their throwing themselves on our protection, divide off their tribal units, and keep them captive in the Yen and Yü parts of Ho Nan, dispersing their habitations over the prefectures and districts, each of which ought to make them cultivate and weave:—by this means a million Tartar freebooters could be transformed into ordinary population, and whilst China would have the advantage of extra numbers, the parts north of the Wall might be steadily kept unpopulated. However the *Chung-shu-ling* Wên Yen-poh recommended that the precedent of the Kien-wu period of Han (A.D. 25–55) should be followed, when the surrendered Hiung-nu were quartered below the Wall at Wu-yüan, thus preserving the whole of the tribal units as a sort of protecting buffer, whilst at the same time they were not parted from their autochthonous ways. 'By following up the occasion and conciliating them, in the first place a wilderness is populated, and on the other hand proof is given of a certain confidence in them. If we send them to Ho Nan Yen-yü, we run counter to their natural inclinations, which is certainly not the way to take care of and cherish them.' T'si-tsung was about to follow this advice, when the *mi shu kien*

Wei Chêng memorialised to the effect that never from ancient times till now had the Turks been in such a battered condition as at the present moment. 'This means that Heaven above had eradicated them, and that the shades of the [dynasty's] ancestors have inspired our arms. Moreover these attacks generation after generation upon China have caused a feeling of intense hatred in our people. Should your Majesty be unable to kill them to extermination now that they have given in their submission, at any rate it is back *north* of the River to which they should be sent, to inhabit their former territory. The Hiung-nu with human exterior possess beasts' minds, and are not of a kind with us. When strong, they are as bound to raid and plunder as, when weak, they are to grovel humbly. They take no heed of kind treatment, for 'tis their nature so. Ts'in and Han suffered from them in the same way, and therefore sent forth brave generals to fight them. Possession was taken of Ho Nan which was turned into prefectures and districts. Why should your Majesty domicile them in the interior? Moreover those have now surrendered approach 100,000: in a few years' time they will have increased a hundredfold. Inhabiting our most central parts, close to the Imperial domain, this malady at our very heart will be a future trouble to us. Least of all it is Ho Nan they should occupy.' Wên Yen-poh memorialised, saying:— 'The Son of Heaven to mankind is "Heaven covering and Earth supporting." Any one coming over to us like this should certainly be cherished. In the present case the remains of the almost annihilated Turks have cast themselves body and soul upon our protection. If your Majesty exhibit no pity or compassion, abandon, and decline to admit them, this will not be "the way of Heaven and Earth," and it will have the effect of discouraging all barbarians. Dense though I be, I protest most strongly against it. To send them to live in Ho Nan would be what is called "bringing the dead to life," "resuscitating the departed": touched by our kindness, they will never rise in revolt.' To this Wei Chêng replied:—'The Tsin dynasty had the Tartar settlements of Wei times distributed over the nearer prefectures. After the subjugation of Wu, Kwoh K'in and Kiang T'ung exhorted the Emperor Wu to chase them away beyond the Wall. The advice of K'in, etc., was not taken and so after a few years they overturned Ch'an-Loh. The overturned cart of former dynasties is not far off as a salutary warning. If you Majesty must needs take Yen-poh's advice and send them to live in Ho Nan, it will be what is called, "cherishing a beast as a legacy of evil for one's self."' To this Wên-poh once more retorted:—'It has been said that the principles of the Sacred Man permeate everywhere, no matter in what direction. The past wise kings of old made no race distinctions in their civilisation. The mere ghosts of the Turks now throw their lives upon us: for us to succour and protect them, taking them in to live in the interior, to receive their directions from us, to be instructed in the rites and the laws, will be after a few years to have them all become agriculturalists. Selections can be made from their chiefs or heads for appointments to serve in the Night Guards. Fearing our power, and feeling our goodness, what trouble can they cause? Kwang-wu domiciled the Southern Shan-yü in the interior prefectures, where he became a Chinese buffer, and for an entire generation there was no rise in revolt.'

Wên-poh being the best arguer, and having hundreds of precedents to cite, it thus came that T'ai-tsung took up his plan, and in the Shoh-fang land from Yu Chou to Ling Chou be established a *tutuh fu* over the four *chou* of Shun, Yu, Hwa, and Ch'ang. Besides he divided Hieh-li's land into six *chou*, the Left being placed under the *tutuh fu* of Ting-siang and the Right under the tutuh fuh of Yü-chung, as commanders of the tribal hordes. Those of the chieftains who came were at once nominated to rank as *tsiang-kün, chung-lang-tsiang*, or such office, with *entrée* according to rank at the Court, fifth rank and over, more than a hundred of them. As a result, those who entered Ch'ang-an to reside numbered several thousand families. Ever since Kieh-shê-shwai's revolt, however, T'ai-tsung had begun to feel uneasy, and besides those who sent up memorials mostly represented that to lodge the Turks in China was really an inconvenient measure, so they were moved to Ho Peh, and the Right Wu-hou Great General, the *tutuh* of Hwa Chou, second-class prince of Hwai-hwa, Sz-me, was set up as the Yih-mi Ni-shuh Hou-li-pi Khagan, and presented with the family surname of Li. He set up his ordo in command of his hordes at Ho Peh.

Study Questions

1. Why was the T'ang emperor in China concerned about anarchy among the Turks out on the steppe?

2. Why, according to the T'ang emperor T'ai-tsung, was the T'ang dynasty refusing to set up the Turkic ruler as khaghan (supreme ruler of the nomads)?

3. What did most officers at the T'ang court in China believe about the Turks after the defeat of Hsieh-li Khan?

4. What did Wei Cheng advise against doing with the surrendered Turkic population?

5. Wen Yen-poh disagreed with Wei Cheng; what was his advice?

6. Whose plan or suggestion did the T'ang emperor adopt? Why?

C. T'ang shu

The passages below from the *T'ang shu* ("T'ang History") are important not for their consideration of contemporary Chinese policy debates towards the Turks but for their evaluations of China's past history in dealing with the nomadic threat. They take a dim view of the Han dynasty's (202 B.C.–A.D. 220) dealings with the Turks. We should note, however, that the T'ang was not significantly more successful in its policy towards the Turks than the Han had been in its policies towards the Hsiung-nu.

The Early Turks

From the *T'ang Shu*

The barbarian nomads have always been a nuisance to China. In former generations the historians have discussed them with great ability. When the T'ang dynasty flourished, the various barbarians were alternately powerful and decrepit. Of those who pretended to equality with China there were four, the Turks, Tibetans, Ouigours, and Yün Nan. At the time in question ministers thronged the court with the recommendations they had to offer. Some were accepted, others ignored, the multiplicity of views being only too apparent. Liu Hwang held then that Yen Yu criticised without being thorough, whilst Pan Ku was thorough without being exhaustive. In the former's comparative search for the best model for a policy he found that the Chou dynasty had adopted the best means, the Ts'in dynasty the next best, and the Han dynasty no effective means at all. On what were his arguments based? The fact that, in the remoteness of half-savage regions where our civilisation does not reach, it is better not to wear out our armies in case the tribes there rebel, nor to abandon a defensive attitude in case they give in their submission. Keep a strict guard, make it difficult for numbers to assemble, and then they will not be able to raid even if they try to do so, or to become our subjects even if they want to: show love for this our China whilst pacifying the four quarters—this was Chou policy: hence we say Chou adopted the best means. The Book of Changes says: 'Princes and Marquesses fortify places in order to strengthen their states,' and the building of Great Walls or the erecting of lines of fortification is what is meant by thus 'fortifying places.' Viscount Kien of Chou raised the Great Wall in order to be ready for the Hu. Yen and Ts'in also built Great Walls in order to draw a line between China and the foreigner. They also arranged citadels and moats. But when the citadels were completed, their state had become extinct, and people lay the blame of it [on this].

Afterwards Wei built a Great Wall. It is said of it that each man had to finish one fathom; that it was 1,000 *li* in extent, and that 300,000 men were employed. After barely a month's work they secured a long respite. Hence the saying that Ts'in adopted the second best means [i.e., Liu Hwang's saying].

The Han dynasty sent a girl of the blood in marriage to the Hiung-nu, yet Kao Tsu had to hold an enquiry into Lu Yüan's not being able to prevent Wang's and Chao's treason, saying that this plan was evidently not the way to put a stop to the Hiung-nu revolts. Moreover Mao-tun assassinated his parent with his own hand, so that surely it was foolish to expect that he would not try his power against that of his grandfather by marriage?

However, the reason a marriage was recommended by those who knew perfectly well it could never bring a lasting peace, was that, as the empire had but recently been conquered, they wished first to quiet down matters of immediate urgency.

In Wu Ti's time China was at peace, and the Hu raids had become rarer. Now was the time for putting an end to them once for all! So, once more were China's resources wasted, and year after year war followed. Hence Yen Yu characterised it as 'doing badly.' Still, up to the time of the Han Emperors Chao and Süan, the troops were well drilled, and the watch-towers were effective. The Hiung-nu kept back, and moved father off. But still we repeated Fêng-ch'un's mistake in going too far, and we emptied our treasuries in order to supply the north-west with 2,700,000 [taels] a year. Virgins of the imperial house served as handmaids in the tent; free men from the imperial court were relegated to the desert. It is submitted that this paying tribute of youths, girls, and local objects is a mark of a vassal's duty! As the Book of Odes says: None dared but to come with offerings; none dared but to come with fealty. That is to say, barbarous regions are supposed to *come* not we to *go*. To publicly enter into a Wu treaty, and then conceal its terms! Why? Because the majesty of the Emperor was dragged into a 'fraternal' alliance with the Hiung-nu, and the name of imperial princess was prostituted to a level with Hu, frumps, incestuous mothers and debauching sons, and following their filthy ways! The difference between China and barbarians lies in the lines we draw between father and son, male and female. For our pretty winsome faces to debase their honour before a strange brood is the acme of dirty humiliation. Yet neither prince nor minister felt the shame of it in Han times, whilst during Wei and Tsin the Tibetans and Tartars occupied the line of the Frontier Wall, and even greater subsidies were paid than before. Every petty chieftain over a hundred men or a thousand souls had presented to him a golden seal and purple ribbon, besides drawing the salary of a prince or marquess. Every horse-herding lad and yak-riding serf who felt disposed to bring his down or his wool, in order to turn a penny by it, came jostling along the roads [as an envoy]. The produce of our fields, the profits of our looms was all scattered about thousands of leagues away from home: the Hu barbarians grew annually more arrogant, whilst Glorious China was daily more oppressed. When they were strong, it cost us all our strength to fight them: when they submitted, they were pampered as before; or, in other words, we nursed them when sick in order that they might attack us when strong! China in short was the humble servant of the K'iang and Hu for about a thousand years. Is not this lamentable? But if we could only transfer all this wealth to the encouragement of our own troops and garrisons, then our people would be rich. If we could only utilise all these honours towards the ingratiation of our responsible officers, then our commanders would be effective. Turn the wealth and the advantage towards ourselves, transfer the danger and the loss to them. No more humiliation in the shape of girls given; no more labour in conveying material. But the Han dynasty rejected this policy: hence they are said to have had no policy at all.

Yen Yu said that the ancients never had a really first-class policy, meaning that we were never able to reduce them to true subjection. As a matter of fact we could, but never tried. Ts'in's 'no policy at all' refers to their driving off the Tartars, but losing their own empire. However their loss of empire was not owing to their expelling the Tartar. Han's attaining a 'poor policy' refers to their attacking the Hu but suffering for it. But if the people had to suffer and in that state to work hard for the enemy's benefit too, that was really the 'no policy at all.' Hence the statement that 'Yen Yu criticised, but not thoroughly.'

Pan Ku said that when they came with loyal intent they should be politely and deferentially received. How so? Politeness and deference are for gentlemen, and not for birds and beasts,—for nomad barbarians. The more fine things are lavished abroad the more covetous the savage heart becomes, and the covetousness of the savage heart is the mainspring of raiding attacks. The sacred man would not join others in enjoying his meals or his music, and when he came to court he took his seat outside the door. The ancients ate in a stooping position so as not to perceive fragrance and delicious flavour. The house of Han were wont to spoil the insolent freebooters teaching them how to appreciate the beauties of Yen and Chao, how to relish the splendid raiment of high dignitaries, and supplying them with brocades and fine silk fabrics for that purpose. The stoppage of grants (which in any case only increased their demands) naturally roused their resentment. It was simply giving ravenous wolves their fill of fine meat and at the same time allowing them to devour what they could take by force themselves. Chinese infantry finds its best account in defensive positions, whilst the freebooters' cavalry do beat on the level plain. If we remain on the strict defensive, we never meet them at all, whereas if we go in pursuit it is merely a helter-skelter race behind them. To defend vital points against them when they choose to come, and to close the same against their return when they choose to go away; to arrest their advance with long spears, to meet them with powerful cross-bows; and not to seek a real victory over them: just as with vermin and reptiles, with whom it were futile to use politeness and deference. And that is what was meant by the statement that 'Pan Ku was thorough without being exhaustive.'

Tu Yu observed that Ts'in, though an insignificant place in Kwan-chung, extinguished six powerful states, and yet now the wealth of the world was exhausted for the behests of the [same] capital. Outside were the currish Tartars domineering us, having already taken several hundred walled places. Inside were wars which had been going on for three years without a moment's peace. Surely it cannot be said that measures of repression now assume a different shape, and that present times are not like these of antiquity? According to the Chou system, 100 paces were a *mu*, and a hundred *mu* were supplied every adult man. When Shang Yang gave his services to Ts'in, he expressed the opinion that the land was not yielding what it should, and allowed 240 paces to a *mu* and a hundred of these *mu* were allowed to each man. And as a good deal of Ts'in land was untilled and the population thin, whilst on the other hand Ts'in's population was too thick for its limits, he enticed over cultivators from the three Ts'in, gave them liberal grants of land and dwellings with exemptions extending to their descendants, and thus enabled Ts'in to hold her own abroad, none but cultivators or fighters being able to hold office. On the average 50 per cent of men were cultivators, and the other 50 per cent, trained fighters. Hence their army was powerful, and their country rich. But, after that, the roads to office grew more numerous, and less worthy means of livelihood became commoner, until at the present day barely 18 per cent, of men are cultivators, the rest all following other industries. Moreover the Chêng Canal of Ts'in and Han irrigated 40,000 *k'ing* of land, whilst the Pêh Canal irrigated 4,500 *k'ing*. During Yung-hwei the two Canals together fructified but 10,000 *k'ing*, whilst at the beginning of Ta-lih this was reduced to 6,000 *mu*, which at a tax of one bushel the *mu* means an annual loss from 4,000,000 to 5,000,000 bushels to the state. When the possibilities of the land and the men are wasted in this way, it is impossible to become rich and powerful. In Han times 700 *li* north of Ch'ang-an the Hiung-nu territory began, and there was never a momentary respite from their predatory attacks. But, when we come to estimate the whole population of the state, we find it did not exceed that of a large Chinese prefecture. Ch'ao Ts'o recommended precautions along the fortified frontier, and consequently the northern lines felt secure. At present the dozen or so of departments west of the T'ung-kwan Pass, east of the Lung Mountains, south of Fu-fang, and north of Chung-nan, contains quite several hundred thousand families. The Tibetans possess neither great power nor much material, they live on scant food, and are clumsy artisans, falling very far short of China. If we could only recover the rich lands around these two Canals, entice over cultivators, to set to work and build citadels and forts in commanding places, by gaining strength through such military colonies we should be able to recover Ho-lung, and need no longer confine ourselves to a defensive attitude.

Yu's grandson Muh also remarked that, when the empire had nothing to disturb it, the great officers lived away in inglorious luxury, whilst fighting men got scattered, arms grew rusty, and ineffective chariots and horses ricketty and weak. The empire grew demoralised, and whenever brigands arose all they had to do was to ride along a clear course in battle against what might be called an 'ever-defeated army.' This was owning to our mistake in not enlisting and drilling, and was reason number one for our checks. For every hundred men who actually bear arms and of course look to government for sustenance there are a thousand names smuggled in, the officers high and low taking the profit on this for themselves and even congratulating themselves on the formidable condition of the freebooters. Those who bear arms are always too few whilst those who consume the food are always too many. Before the mud of the forts is dry, the public chest is empty. This is owing to our mistake in not insisting on reality, and reason number two for our checks. Whenever we get a small victory in battle, a great fuss is made over the service, and over sending messengers to report it, in order to reap the reward for it, sometimes two presents being made in one day, or several promotions in one month. Before the conqueror has returned and heard his triumph sung, he is already gazetted to high rank: he is at the top of the tree; he receives a mansion and fine estate; he is overwhelmed with gold and silks; his descendants receive appointments. Does he ever think of dying abroad and giving his best for us? This is owing to our mistake in over rewarding, and reason number three for our checks. After immense loss in soldiers' lives and the turning upside down of our metropolis, they come skipping here and depart after assassinating their country. As they glance at the knife and the saw, their expression is very calm, and before the year is out they have already taken their stand on the altar steps. This is owing to our mistake in punishing inadequately, and reason number four for our checks. The commander-in-chief is not granted a free hand in his conduct of the campaign: one says it is to be half-moon, another says it is to be fish dropping; as the armies with their tens of thousands deploy and form evolution, the freebooter cavalry pounce upon them just in the moment of their alarm and hurry. This is owing to our mistake in not unifying the command, and reason number five for our checks. During Yüan-ho we musterd several hundred thousand soldiers to punish Ts'ai, in consequence of which the Empire was *saigné à blanc* for four years before we took it, the reason being that all the above faults were in full swing. At the beginning of Ch'ang-ch'u we had our work done for us by the descendants of bandits, but before long the Yen and Chao anarchy arose, ending in five defeats of such discredited generals and armies as we could scrape together, so that we were less able than ever to inspire terror into the rebellious freebooters.

Such being the language of the two Tu, we may add to it that, in Kwang-Teh and Kien-chung, the Tibetans twice watered their horses in the River Min, and used to make use of the Nan-chao as their advance guard, wielding their 20-feet-long lances and alternately fighting and advancing: our Sz Ch'wan soldiers had their swords broken and barbs thrust down their throats without being able to kill a single *Jung*. But the *Jung* soldiers advanced farther day by day, and lost more and more of their men by disease, in consequence of which, seeing that they could not remain, they withdrew of their own accord. The Sz Ch'wan people had a refrain: 'We could manage with the western *Jung*, but the southern barbarians massacre us!' And so on until Wei Ku opened the Ts'ing k'i road, by way of conciliating the various barbarians, causing them to send tribute by way of Sz Ch'wan, and to select youths for instruction at Ch'êng-tu, in reading, writing, and arithmetic. Having completed their course they returned, fully instructed as to our topography and vital points! In Wên Tsung's time they entered as far as Ch'êng-tu in great force, and from Yüeh-si northwards for 800 *li* the country was denuded of both population and beasts, added to which our defeated soldiers and starving populace took the opportunity to kill and plunder, and the officials could do nothing to prevent it. After this the various barbarians again had the idea of ravaging Shuh, and the Shuh people, weary of incessant war-service, were also ready to welcome them in order to escape it. No one who has not served in the field, year in and year out, can have any adequate notion of the difficulties of campaigning. On stage, even of easy marching, makes one groan and sweat, whilst the generals are harsh and self-seeking, changing the good rations of cloth for sleazy stuff, and mixing the rice contributions with sand. Hence the border soldiers were indignantly disappointed, and Pa-Shuh was in a miserable condition. Sun Ts'iao said that the three department of Yüeh-si, Yen-tao, and Ch'ên-li ought to be commanded by decree to find out defensive vital spots, enlist troops, and hold them; also that if soldiers were enlisted locally they would be easier to use, as men taken from the border would also be better acquainted with the defensive points; suitable spots should be selected for colony camps, and the land should be tilled in spring and silk raised in summer in order to supply food and clothing, whilst in autumn and winter they should keep strictly together in arms, in anticipation of raids; that every year an honest officer should be despatched to see if the troops were duly supplied with everything, and in this way the officials would be unable to peculate the stores, whilst the clerks would have no chance to steal them. This, he said, was a defensive plan which was quite capable of being put to force, and it is therefore here recorded as an introduction to our subject, and next come the vicissitudes of Turks, Tibetans, Ouigours, one after the other; after which again the Eastern Barbarians, Western Regions, according to the relative importance of our wars with each. Finally comes the account of the Southern Barbarians, who were the cause of T'ang's downfall.

The A-shï-no (Turk) family was a *northern tribe* of the ancient Hiung-nu, occupying the Southern parts of the Golden Mountains, and vassal to the Juan-juan. Their kind went on increasing, generation by generation, down to T'u-mên, when they became powerful and changed their title to that of 'Khan' which is much as 'Shen-Yü.' The wife was called 'Khatun.' *Their land on three sides extended to the sea,* and south reached to the Great Desert. *The military commands of their separate tribes were called* sbêh. *The youth were styled* t'êh-lêh. *The high officers were called* jabghu, *and* küh-lüh-ohüh *and* apa, *and* sz-li-fah, *and* t'u-t'un *and* sz-kin, *and* yen-hung-tah *and* hieh-li-fah, *and* tah-kan. *28 ranks in all, and each post an hereditary one, but there is no limit to the number of officials. The guards are called* fu-li. *The Khan sets up his court at Tu-kin Mountain, and at the ordo door he erects a standard with a golden wolf's head. It faces always east.*

Study Questions

1. What does this passage say the "barbarian nomads" have always been to China?

2. This passage reviews China's earlier history in dealing with the barbarians. What does it think of the Han dynasty's policy of intermarriage between Chinese and barbarian royal families as a means of securing peace?

3. What does the writer of this passage think of Pan Ku's (a Han historian) strategies for dealing with the nomads?

D. The Uighurs

T he Uighurs, the Turkic cousins of the T'u-chueh, came to power in A.D. 744 after prevailing over them. The Uighurs succeeded in building a capital city in Mongolia named Karabalgasun and in adapting a written script for their language. They were wealthier and, in Chinese eyes, slightly less uncouth than the T'u-chueh had been. They helped the T'ang recover its capital city, Ch'ang-an, in the wake of a devastating internal rebellion in China. The Uighur empire came to an end in 840, when the savage Kirgiz, yet another Turkic people from the far reaches of the Yenesei River in Siberia, looted Karabalgasun and then abandoned it.

The Uighurs endured as a people and in subsequent centuries quit their Buddhist faith for the monotheistic religion of Islam. They are today the single largest ethnic group in China's so-called "autonomous region" of Xinjiang, in northwest China. Many Uighurs today fiercely resent Chinese domination over Xinjiang and would end it if they were able to.

The passages below are excerpted from the *Chiu T'ang shu* ("Old T'ang History") and the *Hsin T'ang shu* ("New T'ang History").

The Uighur Empire
According to the T'ang Dynastic Histories
Colin Mackerras, Editor and Translator

In the tenth month (16/11–15/12/757), the Prince of Kuang-p'ing and the Deputy Generalissimo, Kuo Tzu-i, led the Uighur soldiers and horses to do battle with the rebels to the west of Shan-chou.

Before this, they had camped at Ch'ü-wo. *Yeh-hu* had sent his general *Chü-pi-shih t'u-po p'ei-fu* and others to go along the side of a southern mountain and then to go east and meet some rebel soldiers who were lying in wait in the valley. The general had completely exterminated these rebels.

Tzu-i had arrived in Hsin-tien, where he came upon a rebel army prepared for battle. He retreated several *li*. The Uighurs saw what was happening, and, crossing over the western slopes of the mountain, they carried aloft their white banners and hastened to attack. They appeared directly at [the rebels'] rear and the rebel hordes suffered a great defeat. Their armies went north, but were trapped or pursued for over twenty *li*. Men and horses were falling over and trampling on one another. There was an incalculable number of dead with more than 100,000 severed heads and corpses lying on the ground for thirty *li* (30/11/757).

The rebel band led by Yen Chuang sent a mounted courier to inform An Ch'ing-hsü what had happened. The latter abandoned (1/12/757) the Eastern Capital [Lo-yang] and fled north at the head of his band, fording the Yellow River. *Yeh-hu* followed the Prince of Kuang-p'ing and the Vice President, Kuo Tzu-i, into the Eastern Capital.

Before this, when they had retaken the Western Capital, the Uighurs had wanted to go into the city and pillage it, but had been firmly prevented by the Prince of Kuan-p'ing. But now, when they retook the Eastern Capital, the Uighurs immediately went into the treasure-houses, and took rich goods from the markets, the villages and city-wards. Their violent robbery lasted three days before it was stopped, and the quantity of goods [plundered] was immeasurable. The Prince of Kuang-p'ing also rewarded them with embroidered hair-cloth and precious stones. *Yeh-hu* was extremely pleased. Su-tsung had returned (8/12/757) to the Western Capital, and in the eleventh month, on the day *kuei-yu*, *Yeh-hu* arrived [at Ch'ang-an] from the Eastern Capital (14/12/757).

By imperial order, the officials had come (14/12/757) to Ch'ang-lo Postal Station to welcome him. The emperor sat in the Grand Audience Hall [to receive him] and gave him a banquet and rewards. *Yeh-hu*, went up into the hall and his other chiefs were arrayed below the steps. The emperor bestowed upon them embroidered many-coloured silken fabrics, and gold and silver utensils. Furthermore, when they bade farewell before returning to their native country, the emperor spoke to them saying, 'That we have been able, on behalf of our state, to undertake a great operation and to bring to completion a righteous and brave work, is owing to your strength.' *Yeh-hu* sent up a memorial saying, 'The Uighur soldiers for battle will stay at Sha-yüan. But now I must go back to Ling-chou and Hsia-chou to collect some horses. Then we can retake Fan-yang and fight and destroy the remaining rebels.'

On the day *chi-ch'ou* (30/12/757), the emperor issued an edict which ran:

> His [*Yeh-hu's*] merit has relieved our fearful difficulties, and his righteousness has made the survival of our state possible. Among distant countries, 10,000 *li* off, only he has had the virtue to be one with us in intention and to save the state. His virtue is unparalleled in ancient or modern times. The Uighur *Yeh-hu* is outstanding for his brave temperament, his pre-eminent birth and his rare gift in strategy. His words are always loyal and trustworthy, and the manifestations of his behaviour are gentle and good. His ability is the equal of that of 10,000 normal men. In rank he must be rated the first of all the barbarians. When cruel and perverted people confused the normal rules [of our state], and China was not yet at peace, the khaghan made an agreement with the state to act as its junior in a partnership of brothers. He made the armies of the father and son [Su-tsung and the Prince of Kuang-p'ing] prosper, he pushed forward his wise stratagems and fought those cruel rebels. 'With one beat of the drum, he excited the spirit of all; having come from 10,000 *li* away, he defeated the enemy, and within twenty days the two capitals were conquered. His resolute strength was enough to pick up the peaks of mountains, and his intelligence was equal to penetrating the winds and clouds. Even in the face of urgent difficulties, he never overstepped his status. To be sure, [his merits are as brilliant as] the sun and moon hanging [in the sky] and [stories about him] shall be told and retold to our descendants. But would it be sufficient to bestow an enfeoffment of land on him for his service and pledge an oath by the Great River that I shall reward him? Among positions the most eminent is the Director of Public Works and among titles the highest is the enfeoffed prince. Therefore I make him a Director of Public Works and I accordingly enfeoff him as 'Chung-i' Prince. Every year there are to be sent for him to the Shuo-fang Army 20,000 rolls of silk, and it is fitting that he should send an embassy to receive this gift.

On the day *jen-shen*, the first day of the fifth month of the first year of Ch'ien-yüan (11/6/758), eighty Uighur envoys, including To-hai *a-po*, and six Abbasid Arab chiefs, including Ko-chih, came simultaneously to court to have audience. When they arrived at the pavilion gate, they argued over who should go in first. The visitors' and audience officials separated them into right and left and they entered at the same time through the east and west gates.

In the sixth month, on the day *wu-hsü*, there was a banquet in honour of some Uighur envoys in front of the Tzu-ch'en Hall (7/7/758).

In the autumn, on the day *ting-hai* of the seventh month (25/8/758), the emperor issued an edict that one of his young daughters should be enfeoffed as the Princess of Ning-kuo, and that she should go out and be married [to the Uighur khaghan]. On the day of her departure for the Uighur territory, the emperor's younger cousin on his father's side, who was the Prefectural Prince of Han-chung, Yü, was to be specially promoted to be Trial President of the Court of Imperial Sacrifices, was to hold temporarily the rank of President of the Censorate, and was to fill the office of Commissioner Who Appoints and Names 'Ying-wu wei-yüan' p'i-chia Khaghan. The emperor's nephew on his father's side, the Left Secretary Sun, as Secretary of the Ministry of War, was to be given temporarily the rank of Vice

President of the Censorate and President of the Court of Diplomatic Reception, and to act as deputy to Yü. Concurrently, [Sun] was to be made the Commissioner for the Rites and Entertainments of the [Wedding of the] Princess of Ning-kuo. The emperor especially sent the senior minister, *K'ai-fu i-t'ung-san-ssu* and Expeditionary Right Vice President of the Department of Affairs of State, the Duke of Chi State, P'ei Mien, to escort them as far as the beginning of the frontier.

On the day *kuei-ssu* (31/8/758), the emperor appointed and set up 'Ying-wu wei-yüan' *p'i-chia* Khaghan of the Uighurs. He sat in the Grand Audience Hall, and the Prince of Han-chung, Yü, received from him the imperial diploma.

On the day *chia-wu* (1/9/758), the Emperor Su-tsung, escorting the Princess of Ning-kuo, arrived at the Tz'u-men Postal Station in Hsien-yang. The princess wept and spoke to him saying, 'The affairs of our state are serious. Even should I die, I shall not regret going.' The emperor shed tears and returned.

When Yü reached his royal camp, *P'i-chia ch'üeh* Khaghan, dressed in a yellow-ochre robe and a barbarian hat, was sitting in his tent on a bed. His insignia and body-guards were extremely abundant. They led Yü before him, standing him outside the tent. The khaghan spoke to Yü saying, 'Prince, what relation are you to the Heavenly Khaghan?' Yü said, 'I am the cousin of the Son of Heaven of T'ang.' Again the khaghan asked, 'Who is it who is standing above you, the prince?' Yü replied, 'It is the palace eunuch Lei Lu-chün.' The khaghan again declared thus, 'The palace eunuch is a slave in status. How is it that he can stand above you, who are of noble birth?' Lei Lu-chün was afraid, he stepped aside and made himself lower.

Everybody was in his proper place. But Yü would not bow and remained standing. The khaghan declared thus, 'The leaders, nobility and subjects of both our states observe a rite. How can you not bow?' Yü said, 'The Son of Heaven of T'ang considered you, the khaghan, to have merit, and therefore he is having his daughter brought here and given to you in marriage. He is tying together a friendship through this marriage with you, the khaghan. Recently the women whom China has given to outside barbarians as wives have in all cases been [merely] daughters of members of the imperial clan and have been named princesses. The present Princess of Ning-kuo is the true daughter of the Son of Heaven. Also she has talents and a becoming appearance and has come 10,000 *li* to be married to the khaghan. The khaghan is to be the son-in-law of the Son of Heaven of the T'ang family. He should know the differences in grades of the rites. How can he conceivably remain seated on his bed while receiving the diploma of such an edict?' At that the khaghan stood up to take the edict and immediately received the imperial diploma of his appointment.

The following day the princess was appointed the khatun. The barbarian chief rejoiced over it and said, 'The Son of Heaven of the T'ang state is most high and has had his true daughter brought here.' The state seals, the silken fabrics, the multi-coloured clothes and garments and the gold and silver dishes which Yü had brought, the khaghan distributed down to the last one among his officials, chiefs, and others. When Yü was on the point of going home, the khaghan presented him with 500 horses and 100 pieces of sable fur.

Study Questions

1. What were the Uighurs allowed to do to Loyang, the Eastern Capital of the T'ang, after recapturing it from internal Chinese rebels?

2. How did the T'ang emperor reward Yeh-hu, the Uighur leader?

3. What was the role and fate of the T'ang emperor's daughter, Princess of Ning-kuo?

VI.

The Mongols

E veryone has heard of Genghis Khan (also spelled Jenghiz Khan or, most correctly, Chinggis Khan). Born in the mid 1100s, Chinggis Khan ultimately led his tiny tribe, the Mongols, to overlordship and absolute power in what we now call Mongolia and much of the rest of the Eurasian world as well.

Chinggis Khan died an old man in 1227, perhaps at the hands of a female assassin. The sons and grandsons who succeeded him built up the greatest empire the world has ever known. In 1280 his grandson Khubilai reigned as supreme ruler (*khan* or *khaghan* in Mongolian) over an empire that encompassed China, Central Asia, Persia, and Russia. In terms of its surface area, the Mongolian world empire was the largest empire the world has ever known.

During the thirteenth century, the period of Mongolian dominance of Eurasia, several Europeans were able to travel safely all the way to Mongolia and China along overland routes. Several Islamic writers and historians also commented on the Mongols and their mighty empire; some clearly detested the Mongols, while others were quite frank in their admiration for the Mongols' leaders and accomplishments.

A. Ibn al-Athīr

I bn al-Athīr (Izz al-Din Abu al-Hasan Ali) was born in Mosul, Iraq in 1160. He is well known in the Islamic world for his great work *al-Kamil*, an annalistic history of the world from its creation to A.D. 1231, the year before his death. He clearly deplores Chinggis Khan's devastation of the Islamic states in Central Asia from 1218 to 1221, as the passage below makes obvious.

The Mongol Invasion and the Muslims

Ibn al-Athīr

... For several years—writes the author Ibn al-Athīr—I put off reporting this event. I found it terrifying and felt revulsion at recounting it and therefore hesitated again and again. Who would find it easy to describe the ruin of Islam and the Muslims? ... O would that my mother had never borne me, that I had died before and that I were forgotten! Though so many friends urged me to chronicle these [events], I still waited. Eventually I came to see that it was no use not complying. The report comprises the story of a ... tremendous disaster such as had never happened before, and which struck all the world, though the Muslims above all. If anyone were to say that at no time since the creation of man by the great God had the world experienced anything like it, he would only be telling the truth. In fact nothing comparable is reported in past chronicles. The worst they recall is the treatment and extinction of the Israelites and the destruction of Jerusalem by Nebuchadnezzar. But what is Jerusalem compared with the areas devastated by those monsters, where every city is twice the size of Jerusalem? What are the Israelites in comparison with [the number of] those they massacred, for a single city whose inhabitants were murdered numbered more than all the Israelites together. It may well be that the world from now until its end ... will not experience the like of it again, apart perhaps from Gog and Magog. Dadjdjāl [the Muslim equivalent of Antichrist] will at least spare those who adhere to him, and will only destroy his adversaries. These [the Mongols], however, spared none. They killed women, men and children, ripped open the bodies of the pregnant and slaughtered the unborn. Truly: we belong to God and shall return to him; only with him is strength and power!

Now, then, to report how the sparks [from these events] flew in all directions, and the evil spread everywhere. It moved across the lands like a cloud before the wind. A people set out from China, overran those fair lands of Turkestan, Kashgar and Balāsāghän, and advancing into Transoxiana toward Samarkand and Bukhara, took them and dealt with their inhabitants in a way which we will recount later. Then one detachment advanced to Khurasan and plundered, devastated, killed and ravaged [the inhabitants] in every way imaginable. After that they pushed toward Rayy [to the east of modern Tehran], Hamadan, into the [Zagros] mountains and on to the threshold of Iraq. Then they turned to Azerbaijan and Arrān, devastated these [areas] and killed the majority of the inhabitants. Only here and there could someone save himself and escape. In less than one year things happened the like of which [until then] had never been heard.

When they had finished with Azerbaijan and Arran they moved toward Derbent in Shirvan and conquered its cities; only the castle where their king was staying saved itself. On they moved into the country where the Alans [=Ossetians] and Lezghians lived, together with other tribes; they overran them, robbing, looting and laying waste. Eventually they invaded the country of the Qipchaq, one of the most numerous Turkish peoples, crushing all who tried to stand in their way. Those remaining fled to the swamps and mountains, and abandoned their land which the

Tatars occupied. All this they did in the shortest imaginable time: they did not stop any longer than was necessary for further advance.

Another detachment turned toward Ghazna [=Ghazni, in present-day eastern Afghanistan] and its surrounding area, and moved on into the neighboring areas of India, to Seistan [Sijistān] and Kerman. They behaved here in the same way as their fellows, perhaps even worse. Never had anything like it been heard of. Even Alexander [the Great] who all sources agree in saying was the ruler of the world, did not come to dominate it so rapidly, but needed ten years to do so: he did not kill anyone, but was content with the submission of the people. But in just one year they [the Mongols] seized the most populous, the most beautiful, and the best cultivated part of the earth whose inhabitants excelled in character and urbanity. In the countries that have not yet been overrun by them, everyone spends the night afraid that they may appear there, too. Incidentally, they do not need a baggage train or stores, since they have with them sheep, horses and other animals, and live exclusively off their meat. The animals on which they ride as they advance pound the earth with their hooves and eat the roots of plants; barley is unknown to them [as fodder]. This is the reason why [the Mongols] do not need any supplies when in camp.

Their religion consists in the adoration of the rising sun. They regard no [food] as forbidden and thus eat any animal, even dogs, pigs and the like. They do not know marriage, and several men will go with one woman; if a child is born, it does not know its father.

Thus Islam and the Muslims were struck, at that time, by a disaster such as no people had experienced before. Part of this was due to those accursed Tatars. They came from the East and committed actions that anybody upon hearing will consider horrifying. God willing, you will now learn about them in detail. Part of this [disaster] is also due to the intrusion into Syria of the cursed Franks [=crusaders] from the West, their attack on Egypt, and their conquest of the coastal strip of Damietta. They might even have seized Egypt and Syria had it not been for God's grace and his help against them [as mentioned earlier]!

. . . May God grant victory to Islam and the Muslims, for he is the most powerful help and support of Islam. If God wishes to inflict harm on a people, there is no way of averting it, and no one but he can intercede. The Tatars succeeded in their advance only because of the lack of any defense. This was due to the fact that the Khwārizm-Shāh Muhammad [II; from 1200] after having conquered the [Iranian] countries had killed and annihilated their rulers. Therefore he alone was left. When he had fled, there remained nobody in these countries who could have defended and protected them. God has only to lay his plans, and already the reality begins to take shape. Now we shall report everything as it happened.

(Ibn al-Athīr, *Chronicon, quod perfectissimum inscribitur*, ed. K.J. Tornberg [12 vols.; Leiden, 1851–76], XII, 233–5)

Study Questions

1. What does Ibn al-Athīr find so distressing to record?
2. Why, according to Ibn al-Athīr, did the Mongols not need any camp supplies or baggage trains?
3. What does Ibn al-Athīr say about Mongolian marriage? Does this tally with what you have already read about Mongolian marriage?

B. Ch'iu Ch'u-chi

In 1222 the Chinese Taoist monk Ch'iu Ch'u-chi set out on a long journey to Afghanistan at the behest of Chinggis Khan, who had issued invitations to the Taoists to come and teach him in the ways of Taoism. The record kept of the journey has survived, and it is now available in English translation. Its author limits most of his record to other matters, but he does occasionally allow himself some observations on the Mongols and their way of life. One such description is given in the brief excerpt below.

Mediaeval Researches from Eastern Asiatic Sources

E. Bretschneider, M.D.

The population was numerous, all living in black carts and white tents. The people are engaged in breeding cattle and hunting. They dress in furs and skins, and live upon milk and flesh-meat.

The men and unmarried young women plait their hair so that it hangs down over their ears. The married women put on their heads a thing made of bark of trees, two feet high, which they sometimes cover with woollen cloth, or, as the rich used to do, with red silk stuff. This cap is provided with a long tail, which they call *gu-gu*, and which resembles a goose or duck. They are always in fear that somebody might have inadvertently run against this cap. Therefore, when entering a tent, they are accustomed to go backward, inclining their heads.

These people (the Mongols) have no writing. They settle their matters by verbal convention, and when they enter into contracts they cut certain marks on wood. They are never disobedient to orders, and never break their word. They have preserved the customs of the early ages.

Study Questions

1. How does the author describe the shelter and food of the Mongols?
2. According to the author, the Mongols had no writing. How then did they enter into contracts?

C. Carpini[3]

John of Plano Carpini, who derives his name from Piano di Carpini near Perugia, was a man of ripe age who had taken a leading part in the establishment of the Franciscan Order in Western Europe. He was chosen Guardian of the new province of Saxony in 1222. In 1228 he became Provincial of Germany. In 1230 he was sent to Spain as Provincial, but in 1233 he returned to Saxony as Provincial. His companion, Brother Giordino di Giano, the chronicler, describes him as "Ordinis sui dilatator maximus", sending Friars all over Northern and Eastern Europe, to Bohemia, Poland, Hungary, Denmark and Norway, watching over the brethren, as a hen over her chicks, and standing "constanter et personaliter" before bishops and princes in defence of his Order. Since he was a corpulent man he used to ride an ass, "and the men of those days were moved by greater devotion towards his ass—on account of the humility of the rider and the newness of the Order—than they are nowadays by the assiduity of the Friars towards the persons of the Ministers". After his return from the Mongol mission we get a vivid picture of him in the pages of Fra Salimbene who met him near Lyons, after he had made his report to Pope Innocent IV. Salimbene says that he often heard him describe his experiences, and when he was tired of talking he would have his book read aloud and would explain any points that his hearers did not understand. Salimbene says that he was well received by the Great Khan and treated honourably and courteously.

On his return the Pope sent Brother John on a mission to St. Louis and in 1248 he was made Archbishop of Antivari in Dalmatia. But his last years were unhappy. He became involved in a serious conflict with the Archbishop of Ragusa on questions of jurisdiction, and he died on August 1st, 1252, while this case was still being tried by the Roman Curia.

John of Plano Carpini's book was by far the most widely known of all the early accounts of Mongols. This is due to the fact that it was incorporated by Vincent of Beauvais in his *Speculum Historiale*, which was one of the most popular encyclopaedic works of the Middle Ages. Vincent was a Dominican who was closely connected with the family of St. Louis and was lector at the royal foundation of Royaumont in the middle of the thirteenth century. As John himself notes at the close of his work, there are two versions of the *History of the Mongols*, a longer and a shorter one, and both survive in a number of MSS. The best MS. and the longer version, on which Fr. van den Wyngaert's printed text is based, is the Corpus Christi, Cambridge, MS. 181, which also contains one of the few surviving texts of William of Rubruck's *Itinerary*. This MS. originally belonged to St. Mary's Abbey at York.

---

3. Christopher Dawson, ed., *The Mongol Mission: Narratives and Letters of the Franciscan Missionaries in Mongolia and China in the Thirteenth and Fourteenth Centuries* (Sheed & Ward Inc., 1955).

History of the Mongols
John of Plano Carpini

Prologue

Friar John of Plano Carpini, of the Order of Friars Minor, envoy of the Apostolic See to the Tartars and other nations of the east, to all the faithful of Christ to whom this present writing may come, the grace of God be to you in this present life and glory in the world to come and a triumphant victory over the enemies of God and of Our Lord Jesus Christ.

When by command of the Apostolic See we went to the Tartars and the other oriental nations, knowing the desire of the Lord Pope and the venerable Cardinals, we chose first to make our way to the Tartars, for we were afraid that in the near future the Church of God would be threatened by danger from that quarter. And although we feared we might be killed by the Tartars or other people, or imprisoned for life, or afflicted with hunger, thirst, cold, heat, injuries, and exceeding great trials almost beyond our powers of endurance—all of which, with the exception of death and imprisonment for life, fell to our lot in various ways in a much greater degree than we had conceived beforehand—nevertheless we did not spare ourselves in order to carry out the will of God as laid down in the Lord Pope's mandate, and be of some service to Christians, that, at all events, having learned the truth about the desire and intention of Tartars, we could make this known to the Christians; then if by chance they made a sudden attack they would not find the Christian people unprepared (as happened on another occasion on account of the sins of men) and inflict a great defeat on them.

Therefore whatever, with your welfare in mind, we shall write to you to put you on your guard, you ought to believe all the more confidently inasmuch as we have either seen everything with our own eyes, for during a year and four months and more we travelled about both through the midst of them and in company with them and we were among them, or we have heard it from Christians who are with them as captives and are, so we believe, to be relied upon. For we had instructions from the Supreme Pontiff to examine everything and to look at everything carefully, and this we zealously carried out, both I and Friar Benedict the Pole of the same Order, who was our companion in our tribulations and our interpreter.

But if for the attention of our readers we write anything which is not known in your parts, you ought not on that account to call us liars, for we are reporting for you things we ourselves have seen or have heard from others whom we believe to be worthy of credence. Indeed it is a very cruel thing that a man should be brought into ill-repute by others on account of the good that he has done.

Chapter I

The Land of the Tartars, Its Position, Physical Features and Climate

Since therefore we wish to write an account of the Tartars in such a way that the reader can easily find his way about it, we will arrange it in chapters as follows. In the first we will speak of the country, in the second of the people, in the third of their religion, [and] in the fourth, of their customs. . . .

We propose treating of the country in this manner: in the first place we will say something of its position, secondly we will speak of its physical features, and thirdly of the nature of the climate there.

Now the aforesaid country lies in that part of the east where, so we believe, the east joins the north. To the east of it lies the country of the Kitayans and also that of the Solangi; to the south the land of the Saracens; to the south-west there is the territory of the Uigurs; to the west the province of the Naimans; on the north it is bounded by the ocean.

In some parts the country is extremely mountainous, in others it is flat, but practically the whole of it is composed of very sandy gravel. In some districts there are small woods, but otherwise it is completely bare of trees. They cook their food and they all, the Emperor as well as the nobles and other men, sit at a fire made of the dung of oxen and horses. Not one hundredth part of the land is fertile, nor can it bear fruit unless it be irrigated by running water, and brooks and streams are few there, and rivers very rare. And so there are no towns or cities there with the exception of one which is said to be quite big and is called Caracarom. We however did not see it, but we were as near as half-a-day's journey to it when we were at the Syra Orda, which is the largest of the camps of their Emperor. Although the land is otherwise barren, it is fit for grazing cattle; even if not very good, at least sufficiently so.

The weather there is astonishingly irregular, for in the middle of summer, when other places are normally enjoying very great heat, there is fierce thunder and lightning which cause the death of many men, and at the same time there are very heavy falls of snow. There are also hurricanes of bitterly cold winds, so violent that at times men can ride on horseback only with great effort. When we were before the orda—that is what the camps of the Emperor and chief men are called—we lay prostrate on account of the force of the wind and we could scarcely see owing to the great clouds of dust. There it never rains in the winter, but often in the summer, though it is so little that sometimes the dust and the roots of the grass are hardly moistened. Very heavy hail also often falls there. At the time when the Emperor was elected and was to be enthroned and we were in the orda, there was such a heavy hailstorm that as a result of its sudden melting, so we clearly understood, more than a hundred and sixty men in that camp were drowned, and many dwellings and much property were washed away. Then also in summer there is suddenly great heat, and suddenly extreme cold. In winter in some parts there are heavy falls of snow, in others however but slight.

To conclude briefly about this country: it is large, but otherwise—as we saw with our own eyes, for during five and a half months we travelled about it—it is more wretched than I can possibly say.

Chapter II

Of Their Persons, Their Clothes, Their Dwelling-Places, Possessions and Marriage

Having spoken of the country, it is now for us to speak of the people. First we will describe their personal appearance, secondly we will add something about their marriages, thirdly their clothes, fourthly their dwellings, and fifthly their possessions.

In appearance the Tartars are quite different from all other men, for they are broader than other people between the eyes and across the cheek-bones. Their cheeks also are rather prominent above their jaws; they have a flat and small nose, their eyes are little and their eyelids raised up to the eyebrows. For the most part, but with a few exceptions, they are slender about the waist; almost all are of medium height. Hardly any of them grow beards, although some have a little hair on the upper lip and chin and this they do not trim. On the top of the head they have a tonsure like clerics, and as a general rule all shave from one ear to the other to the breadth of three fingers, and this shaving joins on to the aforesaid tonsure. Above the forehead also they all likewise shave to two fingers' breadth, but the hair between this shaving and the tonsure they allow to grow until it reaches their eyebrows and, cutting more from each side of the forehead than in the middle, they make the hair in the middle long; the rest of their hair they allow to grow like women, and they make it into two braids which they bind, one behind each ear. They also have small feet.

Each man has as many wives as he can keep, one a hundred, another fifty, another ten—one more, another less. It is the general custom for them to marry any of their relations, with the exception of their mother, daughter and sister by the same mother. They can however take in marriage their sisters who have only the same father, and even their father's wives after his death; also a younger brother may marry his brother's wife after his death; or another younger relation is expected to take her. All other women they take as wives without any distinction and they buy them at a very high price from their parents. After the death of their husbands the women do not easily enter into a second union, unless a man wishes to take his stepmother to wife.

The clothes of both the men and the women are made in the same style. They do not use capes, cloaks or hoods, but wear tunics of buckram, velvet or brocade made in the following fashion: they are open from top to bottom and are folded over the breast; they are fastened on the left with one tie, on the right with three, on the left side also they are open as far as the waist. Garments of all kinds of fur are made in the same style; the upper one however has the hairy part outside and is open at the back; it also has a tail at the back reaching to the knees.

The married women have a very full tunic, open to the ground in front. On their head they have a round thing made of twigs or bark, which is an ell in height and ends on top in a square; it gradually increases in circumference from the bottom to the top, and on the top there is a long and slender cane of gold or silver or wood, or even a feather, and it is sewn on to a cap which reaches to the shoulders. The cap as well as this object is covered with buckram, velvet or brocade, and without this head-gear they never go into the presence of men and by it they are distinguished from other women. It is hard to tell unmarried women and young girls from men, for they are dressed in every respect like them. The caps they have are different from those of other nations, but I am unable to describe what they are like in such a way as you would understand.

Their dwelling-places are round like tents and are made of twigs and slender sticks. At the top in the middle there is a round opening which lets in the light, and is also to enable the smoke to escape, for they always make their fire in the middle. Both the sides and the roof are covered with felt, and the doors also are made of felt. Some of these dwellings are large, others small, according to the importance or significance of the people; some can be speedily taken down and put up again and are carried on baggage animals; others cannot be taken down but are moved on carts. To carry them on a cart, for the smaller ones one ox is sufficient, for the larger ones three, four or even more according to the size. Wherever they go, be it to war or anywhere else, they always take their dwellings with them.

They are extremely rich in animals, camels, oxen, sheep, goats; they have such a number of horses and mares that I do not believe there are so many in all the rest of the world; they do not have pigs or other farm animals.

The Emperor, the nobles and other important men own large quantities of gold and silver, silk, precious stones and jewels.

Chapter III

Of Their Worship of God, Those Things Which They Consider To Be Sins, Divinations and Purifications, Funeral Rites, etc.

Having spoken of the men, we must now add something about their religion, and we will deal with it in this way: first we will speak of their worship of God, next of those things which they believe to be sins, thirdly of divinations and purifications for sins, and fourthly of their funeral rites.

The believe in one God, and they believe that He is the maker of all things visible and invisible; and that it is He who is the giver of the good things of this world as well as the hardships; they do not, however, worship Him with prayers or praises or any kind of ceremony. Their belief in God does not prevent them from having idols of felt made in the image of man, and these they place on each side of the door of the dwelling; below them they put a felt model of an udder, and they believe that these are the guardians of the cattle and grant them the benefit of milk and foals; yet others they make out of silken materials and to these they pay great honour. Some put them in a beautiful covered cart before the door of their dwelling and if anyone steals anything from that cart he is put to death without any mercy. When they wish to make these idols, all the chief ladies in the different dwellings meet together and reverently make them; and when they have finished they kill a sheep and eat it and burn its bones in the fire. Also when any child is ill they make an idol as I have described and fasten it above his bed. Chiefs, captains of a thousand men and captains of a hundred, always have a shrine [hercium] in the middle of their dwelling.

They always offer to their idols the first milk of every cow and mare. When they are going to eat and drink they first make an offering to them of some of the food and drink. When they kill any animal they offer its heart in a cup to the idol in the cart; they leave it there until the morning, when they remove it from its presence, cook it and eat it. They have also made an idol to the first Emperor, which they have placed in a cart in a place of honour before a dwelling, as we saw before the present Emperor's court, and they offer many gifts to it; they also present horses to it and no one dare mount these till their death; they also give other animals to it, and if they slaughter these for food they do not break any of their bones but burn them in a fire. They bow to it towards the south as to God, and they make other nobles who are visiting them do the same.

Whence it recently came about that when Michael, one of the chief dukes of Russia, came on a visit to Bati, they made him first pass between two fires. After that they told him to bow towards the south to Chingis Chan; he replied that he would gladly bow to Bati and his attendants but he would not make an inclination to the image of a dead man, for it was not lawful for Christians to do this. When they had told him many times that he was to bow and he would not, the chief Bati sent him word through the son of Jaroslaus that if he did not bow he would be put to death. He answered that he would rather die than do what was not lawful. Bati sent one of his attendants who went on kicking him in the stomach against his heart until he began to weaken. Thereupon one of his soldiers who was standing by encouraged him, saying "Be constant, for this suffering will last but a short time and eternal joy will follow hard upon it." Then they cut off his head with a knife, and the soldier also was beheaded.

In addition they venerate and adore the sun, the moon, fire, water and the earth, making them the first offerings of food and drink, especially in the morning before they eat or even drink. Since they observe no law with regard to the worship of God they have up to now, so we understood, compelled no one to deny his faith or law with the exception of Michael of whom we have just spoken. What they may ultimately do we do not know, but there are some who are of the opinion that, if they became sole rulers, which God forbid, they would make everyone bow down to that idol.

During our stay in the country it happened that Andrew, Duke of Cherneglone which is in Russia, was accused before Bati of taking Tartar horses out of the country and selling them elsewhere; and although the charge was not proved he was put to death. Hearing this, his younger brother came with the widow of the slain man to the chief Bati to petition him not to take away their territory from them. Bati told the boy to take the widow of the slain man, the boy's own brother, as his wife; and bade the woman take him as her husband according to Tartar custom. She said that she would rather die than break the law. But none the less he gave her to him [as wife], although both of them refused as much as they could. And they put them both to bed together and forced them to consummate the marriage in spite of her tears and cries.

Although they have no law concerning the doing of what is right or the avoidance of sin, nevertheless there are certain traditional things, invented by them or their ancestors, which they say are sins; for example, to stick a knife into a fire, or even in any way to touch fire with a knife, or to extract meat from the cauldron with a knife, or to chop with an axe near a fire; for they believe that, if these things were done, the fire would be beheaded; likewise to lean on a whip with which a horse is lashed, for they do not use spurs: also to touch arrows with a whip; again to catch or kill young birds, to strike a horse with a bridle; also to break a bone with another bone, to pour out upon the ground milk or any kind of drink or food; to pass water inside a dwelling. If a man does this on purpose he is put to death, otherwise he has to pay a large sum of money to the soothsayer, who purifies him and has the dwelling and its contents carried between two fires; but before this purification has been carried out no one dare enter the dwelling or take away anything from it: again, if anyone takes a morsel and, unable to swallow it, spits it out of his mouth, a hole is made under the dwelling and he is dragged out by that hole and without any mercy put to death, also if a man treads on the threshold of a dwelling belonging to any chief he is put to death in the same way. They have many things like this which it would be tedious to tell of.

On the other hand, to kill men, to invade the countries of other people, to take the property of others in any unlawful way, to commit fornication, to revile other men, to act contrary to the prohibitions and commandments of God, is considered no sin by them.

They know nothing of everlasting life and eternal damnation, but they believe that after death they will live in another world and increase their flocks, and eat and drink and do the other things which are done by men living in this world.

They pay great attention to divinations, auguries, soothsayings, sorceries and incantations, and when they receive an answer from the demons they believe that a god is speaking to them. This god they call Itoga—the Comans however call him Kam—and they have a wondrous fear and reverence for him and offer him many oblations and the first portion of their food and drink, and they do everything according to the answers he gives. When the moon is new, or at full moon, they embark on anything fresh they wish to do, and so they call the moon the great Emperor and bend the knee and pray to it. They also say that the sun is the mother of the moon because it receives its light from the sun. They believe, to put it shortly, that everything is purified by fire. Consequently when envoys or princes or any persons whatsoever come to them, they are obliged to pass between two fires, together with the gifts they are bringing, in order to be purified, lest perchance they have practised sorcery or brought poison or anything else injurious. Also if fire falls from heaven on cattle or men, a thing which often happens there, or any similar thing befalls them by which they are considered unclean or unlucky, they have to be purified in the same way by the diviners. They place almost all their hope in such things.

When anyone is sick past cure, they put a spear there and wind black felt round it and from then onwards no outsider dares to enter within the bounds of his dwellings. When the death agony begins almost everybody leaves him, for none of those who are present at his death can enter the orda of any chief or of the Emperor until the new moon.

When he is dead, if he is one of the less important men, he is buried in secret in the open country wherever it seems good to them. He is buried with one of his dwellings, sitting in the middle of it, and they place a table in front of him, and a dish filled with meat and a goblet of mare's milk. And they bury with him a mare and her foal and a horse with bridle and saddle, and another horse they eat and fill its skin with straw, and this they stick up on two or four poles, so that in the next world he may have a dwelling in which to make his abode and a mare to provide him with milk, and that he may be able to increase his horses and have horses on which to ride. The bones of the horse which they eat they burn for his soul; and also the women often assemble to burn bones for the men's souls, as we saw with our own eyes and learned from other there. We also saw that Occodai Chan, the father of the present Emperor, left behind a grove to grow for his soul, and he ordered that no one was to cut there, and anyone who cuts a twig there, as we ourselves saw, is beaten, stripped and maltreated. And when we were in great need of something with which to whip our horse, we did not dare to cut a switch from there. They also bury gold and silver in the same way with a dead man; the cart in which he rides is broken up and his dwelling destroyed, nor does anyone dare to pronounce his name until the third generation.

They have a different method of burying their chief men. They go in secret into the open country and there they remove the grass, roots and all, and they dig a large pit and in the side of this pit they hollow out a grave under the earth; and they put his favourite slave under him. He lies there under the body until he is also at the point of death, then they drag him out to let him breathe, and this they do three times. If the slave escapes with his life, he is afterwards a free man and can do whatever he pleases and is an important man in his master's camp and among his relations. The dead man they place in the grave made in the side along with the things mentioned above. Then they fill the pit in front of his grave, and they put the grass over it as it was before so that no one may be able to discover the spot afterwards. The other things already described they also do, but his tent they leave above ground in the open.

In their country there are two cemeteries. One is where the Emperors, chiefs and all the nobles are interred, and wherever they die they are brought thither if this can fittingly be done. A great deal of gold and silver is buried with them. The other cemetery is the one where lie buried those who were killed in Hungary, for many lost their lives there. No one dare go near these cemeteries except the keepers who have been put there to look after them. If anyone does approach them, he is seized, stripped, beaten and severely maltreated. We ourselves unwittingly entered the bounds of the cemetery of the men who were killed in Hungary, and they bore down upon us and would have shot at us with arrows, but, since we were envoys and did not know the customs of the land, they let us go free.

The relatives of the dead man and all those living in his dwellings have to be purified by fire. This purification is performed in the following manner: they make two fires and they put two spears near the fires, with a rope fastened on to the top of them, on to which they tie strips of buckram; under this rope and its ribbons and between the two fires pass men, animals and dwellings. And there are two women, one this side, the other that, who sprinkle water and recite incantations. If any carts break down there, or if anything falls to the ground on that spot, the enchanters get it. If anyone is killed by a thunderbolt, all the people living in his dwellings have to pass through the fires in the manner described; no one touches his tent, his bed, cart, felt, clothes or any other such things as he had; but they are spurned by all as unclean.

Chapter IV

Of Their Character, Good and Bad, Their Customs, Food, etc.

Having spoken of their religion, now we must speak of their character, which we will deal with in this way: first we will tell of their good points, then of their bad, thirdly of their customs, and fourthly of their food.

These men, that is to say the Tartars, are more obedient to their masters than any other men in the world, be they religious or seculars; they show great respect to them nor do they lightly lie to them. They rarely or never contend with each other in word, and in action never. Fights, brawls, wounding, murder are never met with among them. Nor are robbers and thieves who steal on a large scale found there; consequently their dwellings and the carts in which they keep their valuables are not secured by bolts and bars. If any animals are lost, whoever comes across them either leaves them alone or takes them to men appointed for this purpose; the owners of the animals apply for them to these men and they get them back without any difficulty. They show considerable respect to each other and are very friendly together, and they willingly share their food with each other, although there is little enough of it. They are also long-suffering. When they are without food, eating nothing at all for one or two days, they do not easily show impatience, but they sing and make merry as if they had eaten well. On horseback they endure great cold and they also put up with excessive heat. Nor are they men fond of luxury; they are not envious of each other; there is practically no litigation among them. No one scorns another but helps him and promotes his good as far as circumstances permit.

Their women are chaste, nor does one hear any mention among them of any shameful behaviour on their part; some of them, however, in jest make use of vile and disgusting language. Discord among them seems to arise rarely or never, and although they may get very drunk, yet in their intoxication they never come to words or blows.

Now that the good characteristics of the Tartars have been described, it is time for something to be said about their bad. They are most arrogant to other people and look down on all, indeed they consider them as nought, be they of high rank or low born.

For at the Emperor's court we saw Jerozlaus, a man of noble birth, a mighty duke of Russia, also the son of the King and Queen of Georgia, and many important sultans; the chief also of the Solangi received no fitting honour from them, but the Tartars who were assigned to them, however base-born they were, went ahead of them and always had the first and highest place; indeed they were often obliged to sit behind their backs.

They are quickly roused to anger with other people and are of an impatient nature; they also tell lies to others and practically no truth is to be found in them. At first indeed they are smooth-tongued, but in the end they sting like a scorpion. They are full of slyness and deceit, and if they can, they get round everyone by their cunning. They are men who are dirty in the way they take food and drink and do other things. Any evil they intend to do to others they conceal in a wonderful way so that the latter can take no precautions nor devise anything to offset their cunning. Drunkenness is considered an honorable thing by them and when anyone drinks too much, he is sick there and then, nor does this prevent him from drinking again. They are exceedingly grasping and avaricious; they are extremely exacting in their demands, most tenacious in holding on to what they have and most niggardly in giving. They consider the slaughter of other people as nothing. In short, it is impossible to put down in writing all their evil characteristics on account of the very great number of them.

Their food consists of everything that can be eaten, for they eat dogs, wolves, foxes and horses and, when driven by necessity, they feed on human flesh. For instance, when they were fighting against a city of the Kitayans, where the Emperor was residing, they besieged it for so long that they themselves completely ran out of supplies and, since they had nothing at all to eat, they thereupon took one out of every ten men for food. They eat the filth which comes away from mares when they bring forth foals. Nay, I have even seen then eating lice. They would say, "Why should I not eat them since they eat the flesh of my son and drink his blood?" I have also seen them eat mice.

They do not use table-cloths or napkins. They have neither bread nor herbs nor vegetables nor anything else, nothing but meat, of which, however, they eat so little that other people would scarcely be able to exist on it. They make their hands very dirty with the grease of the meat, but when they eat they wipe them on their leggings or the grass or some other such thing. It is the custom for the more respectable among them to have small bits of cloth with which they wipe their hands at the end when they eat meat. One of them cuts the morsels and another takes them on the point of a knife and offers them to each, to some more, to some less, according to whether they wish to show them greater or less honour. They do not wash their dishes, and, if occasionally they rinse them with meat broth, they put it back with the meat into the pot. Pots also or spoons or other articles intended for this use, if they are cleaned at all, are washed in the same manner. They consider it a great sin if any food or drink is allowed to be wasted in any way; consequently they do not allow bones to be given to dogs until the marrow has been extracted. They do not wash their clothes nor allow them to be washed, especially from the time when thunderstorms begin until the weather changes. They drink mare's milk in very great quantities if they have it; they also drink the milk of ewes, cows, goats and even camels. They do not have wine, ale or mead unless it is sent or given to them by other nations. In the winter, moreover, unless they are wealthy, they do not have mare's milk. They boil millet in water and make it so thin that they cannot eat it but have to drink it. Each one of them drinks one or two cups in the morning and they eat nothing more during the day; in the evening, however, they are all given a little meat and they drink the meat broth. But in the summer, seeing they have plenty of mare's milk, they seldom eat meat, unless it happens to be given to them or they catch some animal or bird when hunting.

They also have a law or custom of putting to death any man and woman they find openly committing adultery; similarly if a virgin commit fornication with anyone, they kill both the man and the woman. If anyone is found in the act of plundering or stealing in the territory under their power, he is put to death without any mercy. Again, if anyone reveals their plans, especially when they intend going to war, he is given a hundred stripes on his back, as heavy as a peasant can give with a big stick. When any of the lower class offend in any way, they are not spared by their superiors, but are soundly beaten. There is no distinction between the son of a concubine and the son of a wife, but the father gives to each what he will; and if they are of a family of princes, then the son of a concubine is a prince just the same as the son of a legitimate wife. When a Tartar has many wives, each one has her own dwelling and her household, and the husband eats and drinks and sleeps one day with one, and the next with another. One, however, is chief among the others and with her he stays more often than with the others. In spite of their numbers, they never easily quarrel among themselves.

The men do not make anything at all, with the exception of arrows, and they also sometimes tend the flocks, but they hunt and practise archery, for they are all, big and little, excellent archers, and their children begin as soon as they are two or three years old to ride and manage horses and to gallop on them, and they are given bows to suit their stature and are taught to shoot; they are extremely agile and also intrepid.

Young girls and women ride and gallop on horseback with agility like the men. We even saw them carrying bows and arrows. Both the men and the women are able to endure long stretches of riding. They have very short stirrups; they look after their horses very well, indeed they take the very greatest care of all their possessions. Their women make everything, leather garments, tunics, shoes, leggings and everything made of leather; they also drive the carts and repair them, they load the camels, and in all their tasks they are very swift and energetic. All the women wear breeches and some of them shoot like the men.

Study Questions

1. Why was John of Plano Carpini sent to the Mongols?
2. John describes "Tartar" land as being unfit for large cities. What was it fit for?
3. What were Mongolian marriage laws like?
4. What is John's description of Mongolian tents?
5. Of what does John disapprove in Mongolian religion?
6. What did the Mongols believe about an afterlife?
7. What were the Mongols' customs for burying their chief men?
8. What were some of the virtues in character that John saw in the Mongols?
9. What were some of their shortcomings, according to John?
10. What did John say of the Mongols' food and eating customs?
11. How did the Mongols deal with the open commitment of adultery?
12. What were the gender roles of Mongolian men?
13. What were the gender roles of Mongolian women?

D. Papal Bulls

In 1241, Mongol armies surrounded Vienna, Austria. It seemed that nothing could stop the Mongols from overrunning and vanquishing all of Christian Europe. The Mongol armies suddenly withdrew late in the year, but Europe was still so unnerved about the prospect of the Mongols' imminent return that Pope Innocent IV dispatched Franciscan friars to the Mongols to rebuke them for their depredations and inquire into their future intentions. With the friars he sent two bulls or messages, translations of which are given below. The first bull is essentially a theological lesson, composed in the apparent hope that the Mongols would, upon reading or hearing it, convert to Christianity or at least respect the Pope and his religious office. The second bull is a peculiar mixture of threats of divine justice and pleas for the Mongols to desist in their invasions.

Two Bulls of Pope Innocent IV

Addressed to the Emperor of the Tartars

I

God the father, of His graciousness regarding with unutterable loving-kindness the unhappy lot of the human race, brought low by the guilt of the first man, and desiring of His exceeding great charity mercifully to restore him whom the devil's envy overthrew by a crafty suggestion, sent from the lofty throne of heaven down to the lowly region of the world His only-begotten Son, consubstantial with Himself, who was conceived by the operation of the Holy Ghost in the womb of a fore-chosen virgin and there clothed in the garb of human flesh, and afterwards proceeding thence by the closed door of His mother's virginity, He showed himself in a form visible to all men. For human nature, being endowed with reason, was meet to be nourished on eternal truth as its choicest food, but, held in mortal chains as a punishment for sin, its powers were thus far reduced that it had to strive to understand the invisible things of reason's food by means of inferences drawn from visible things. The Creator of that creature became visible, clothed in our flesh, not without change in His nature, in order that, having become visible, He might call back to Himself, the Invisible, those pursuing after visible things, moulding men by His salutary instructions and pointing out to them by means of His teaching the way of perfection: following the pattern of His holy way of life and His words of evangelical instruction, He deigned to suffer death by the torture of the cruel cross, that by a penal end to His present life, He might make an end of the penalty of eternal death, which the succeeding generations had incurred by the transgression of their first parent, and that man might drink of the sweetness of the life of eternity from the bitter chalice of His death in time. For it behooved the Mediator between us and God to possess both transient mortality and everlasting beatitude, in order that by means of the transient He might be like those doomed to die and might transfer us from among the dead to that which lasts for ever.

He therefore offered Himself as a victim for the redemption of mankind and, overthrowing the enemy of its salvation, He snatched it from the shame of servitude to the glory of liberty, and unbarred for it the gate of the heavenly fatherland. Then, rising from the dead and ascending to heaven, He left His vicar on earth, and to him, after he had borne witness to the constancy of his love by the proof of a threefold profession, He committed the care of souls, that he should with watchfulness pay heed to and with heed watch over their salvation, for which He had humbled His high dignity; and He handed to him the keys of the kingdom of heaven by which he and, through him, his successors, were to possess the power of opening and closing of the gate of that kingdom to all. Wherefore we, though unworthy, having become, by the Lord's disposition, the successor of this vicar, do turn our keen attention, before all else incumbent on us in virtue of our office, to your salvation and that of other men, and on this matter especially do we fix our mind, sedulously keeping watch over it with diligent zeal and zealous diligence, so that we may be able, with the help of God's grace, to lead those in error into the way of truth and gain all men for Him.

But since we are unable to be present in person in different places at one and the same time—for the nature of our human condition does not allow this—in order that we may not appear to neglect in any way those absent from us we send to them in our stead prudent and discreet men by whose ministry we carry out the obligation of our apostolic mission to them. It is for this reason that we have thought fit to send to you our beloved son Friar Laurence of Portugal and his companions of the Order of Friars Minor, the bearers of this letter, men remarkable for their religious spirit, comely in their virtue and gifted with a knowledge of Holy Scripture, so that following their salutary instructions you may acknowledge Jesus Christ the very Son of God and worship His glorious name by practicing the Christian religion. We therefore admonish you all, beg and earnestly entreat you, to receive these Friars kindly and to treat them in considerate fashion out of reverence for God and for us, indeed as if receiving us in their persons, and to employ unfeigned honesty towards them in respect of those matters of which they will speak to you on our behalf; we also ask that, having treated with them concerning the aforesaid matters to your profit, you will furnish them with a safe-conduct and other necessities on both their outward and return journey, so that they can safely make their way back to our presence when they wish. We have thought fit to send to you the above-mentioned Friars, whom we specially chose out from among others as being men proved by years of regular observance and well versed in Holy Scripture, for we believed they would be of greater help to you, seeing that they follow the humility of our Saviour: if we had thought that ecclesiastical prelates or other powerful men would be more profitable and more acceptable to you we would have sent them.

Lyons, 5ᵗʰ March 1245

Study Questions

1. What was the content of Pope Innocent IV's first bull sent to the "emperor of Tartars"?

2. What does Innocent IV ask of the Mongol khan in this first bull?

II

Seeing that not only men but even irrational animals, nay, the very elements which go to make up the world machine, are united by a certain innate law after the manner of the celestial spirits, all of which God the Creator has divided into choirs in the enduring stability of peaceful order, it is not without cause that we are driven to express in strong terms our amazement that you, as we have heard, have invaded many countries belonging both to Christians and to others and are laying them waste in a horrible desolation, and with a fury still unabated you do not cease from stretching out your destroying hand to more distant lands, but, breaking the bond of natural ties, sparing neither sex nor age, you rage against all indiscriminately with the sword of chastisement. We, therefore, following the example of the King of Peace, and desiring that all men should live united in concord in the fear of God, do admonish, beg and earnestly beseech all of you that for the future you desist entirely from assaults of this kind and especially from the persecution of Christians, and that after so many and such grievous offences you conciliate by a fitting penance the wrath of Divine Majesty, which without doubt you have seriously aroused by such provocation; nor should you be emboldened to commit further savagery by the fact that when the sword of your might has raised against other men Almighty God has, up to the present allowed various nations to fall before your face; for sometimes He refrains from chastising the proud in this world for the moment, for this reason, that if they neglect to humble themselves of their own accord He may not only no longer put off the punishment of their wickedness in this life but may also take greater vengeance in the world to come. On this account we have thought fit to send to you our beloved son [John of Plano Carpini] and his companions the bearers of this letter, men remarkable for their religious spirit, comely in their virtue and gifted with a knowledge of Holy Scripture; receive them kindly and treat them with honour out of reverence for God, indeed as if receiving us in their persons, and deal honestly with them in those matters of which they will speak to you on our behalf, and when you have had profitable discussions with them concerning the aforesaid affairs, especially those pertaining to peace, make fully known to us through these same Friars what moved you to destroy other nations and what your intentions are for the future, furnishing them with a safe-conduct and other necessities on both their outward and return journey, so that they can safely make their way back to our presence when they wish.

Lyons, 13th March 1245

Study Questions

1. What does Innocent IV chastise the Mongolian emperor for?
2. What does Innocent IV "admonish, beg and earnestly beseech" the Mongolian khan to do (or rather not to do)?
3. What threat does Innocent IV offer to the Mongolian khan?
4. What specific question does Innocent IV want answered?

E. Güyük Khan's Responses to the Papal Bulls

G üyük Khan was not at all impressed with the Papal bulls. He found them incomprehensible and, perhaps more importantly, impudent. His response to them was as harsh as it was direct. But in spite of the tone and content of his reply, the Mongols never made serious moves against Europe again. They had much greater prizes in mind: Persia, Mesopotamia, and especially China.

Güyük Khan's Letter to Pope Innocent IV (1246)

We, by the power of the eternal heaven,

>   Khan of the great Ulus

Our command:—

> This is a version sent to the great Pope, that he may know and under-
> stand in the [Muslim] tongue, what has been written. The petition of the
> assembly held in the lands of the Emperor [for our support], has been
> heard from your emissaries.

If he reaches [you] with his own report, Thou, who art the great Pope, together
with all the Princes, come in person to serve us. At that time I shall make known all
the commands of the *Yasa*.

You have also said that supplication and prayer have been offered by you, that I
might find a good entry into baptism. This prayer of thine I have not understood.
Other words which thou hast sent me: "I am surprised that thou hast seized all the
lands of the Magyar and the Christians. Tell us what their fault is." These words of
thine I have also not understood. The eternal God has slain and annihilated these
lands and peoples, because they have neither adhered to Chingis Khan, nor to the
Khagan, both of whom have been sent to make known God's command, nor to the
command of God. Like thy words, they also were impudent, they were proud and
they slew our messenger-emissaries. How could anybody seize or kill by his own
power contrary to command of God?

Though thou likewise sayest that I should become a trembling Nestorian
Christian, worship God and be an ascetic, how knowest thou whom God absolves,
in truth to whom He shows mercy? How dost thou know that such words as thou
speakest are with God's sanction? From the rising of the sun to its setting, all the
lands have been made subject to me. Who could do this contrary to the command
of God?

Now you should say with a sincere heart: "I will submit and serve you." Thou
thyself, at the head of all the Princes, come at once to serve and wait upon us! At that
time I shall recognize your submission.

If you do not observe God's command, and if you ignore my command, I shall
know you as my enemy. Likewise I shall make you understand. If you do otherwise,
God knows what I know.

At the end of Jumada the second in the year 644.

The Seal

We, by the power of the eternal Tengri, universal Khan of the great Mongol
Ulus—our command. If this reaches peoples who have made their submission, let
them respect and stand in awe of it.

Study Questions

1. What was Güyük Khan's response to these two papal bulls?
2. What explanation did Güyük offer for the Mongols' campaigns and slaughter?
3. What rhetorical question did Güyük pose to Innocent IV?
4. What were Güyük's instructions to the Pope?

F. William of Rubruck[4]

Hardly anything is known about this great man except what he tells us in his book. The dates of his birth and his death are unknown, but he seems to have been a much younger man than John of Plano Carpini. It is almost certain that he was a native of Flanders, deriving his name from Rubruc near Cassel, now in French Flanders, not from Ruisbroek in Brabant as has sometimes been supposed.

After his return from Mongolia he was detained by Order in Palestine, as lector in Theology at Acre, and he was obliged to ask St. Louis to obtain permission for his return to Europe. This request was eventually granted, and he came to Paris. Here he met Roger Bacon who was intensely interested in his experiences, and refers to him at length in the *Opus Majus*. This is the last we hear of him. Indeed it is the only contemporary record of him that we possess. But Roger Bacon's account seems to have aroused the interest of his countrymen, for except in England William and his travels were practically forgotten until modern times. The three MSS. at Corpus Christi College, Cambridge, and the one in the British Museum, are the sources of all the existing MSS. and versions and it was in England that Hakluyt and Purchas first published their versions. Thus it is almost by accident that the work of one of the greatest of medieval travellers has survived, and it is only in our own time that the accuracy and historical importance of his work have been fully recognized.

---

4. Christopher Dawson, ed., *The Mongol Mission: Narratives and Letters of the Franciscan Missionaries in Mongolia and China in the Thirteenth and Fourteenth Centuries* (Sheed & Ward Inc., 1955).

The Journey of William of Rubruck

Friar William of Rubruck, least in the Order of Friars Minor, to the most excellent Lord and most Christian Louis, by the grace of God illustrious King of the French, health and continual triumph in Christ.

It is written of the Wise Man in Ecclesiasticus: "He shall pass into strange countries, he shall try good and evil in all things." This have I fulfilled, my Lord King, but would that it were as a wise man and not as a fool: for many perform the same actions as a wise man, not however in a wise manner but rather foolishly, and I fear I am to be numbered among these. Nevertheless, whatever be the manner in which I have acted, since you told me when I took my leave of you that I was to write to you of everything I should see among the Tartars, and even admonished me not to be afraid of writing you a long letter, I am doing what you bade me, albeit with fear and diffidence, for words such as I ought to use when writing to so eminent a majesty do not readily spring to my mind.

Chapter I

The Province of Gazaria

Be it known therefore to your holy Majesty that in the year of Our Lord one thousand two hundred and fifty-three on the seventh of May we entered the Sea of Pontus which is commonly called the Greater Sea. It is one thousand four hundred miles in length, as I learned from merchants, and is divided into two parts, for about the middle of it there are two points of land, one in the north and the other in the south. The one in the south is called Sinopolis [Sinope] and is a fortress and the port of the Sultan of Turkey: as for the one in the north it is that province which is nowadays called Gazaria by the Latins, but by the Greeks who dwell on the sea coast is named Cassaria, that is to say, Caesarea. There are also certain promontories stretching out into the sea towards the south in the direction of Sinopolis. There are three hundred miles between Sinopolis and Cassaria. It is, by and large, seven hundred miles from these points to Constantinople and seven hundred to the east, that is, to Hyberia which is the province of Georgia.

We sailed in the direction of the province of Gazaria or Cassaria, which is like a triangle, on the west side of which lies the city called Kersona [Sebastopol] where St. Clement met his martyrdom. As we sailed by we saw the island on which is the temple said to have been built by the hands of angels. In the middle of the south side, as it were at the apex, there is a city called Soldaia [Sudak], which looks towards Sinopolis, and all the merchants coming from Turkey and wishing to go to northern lands make their way thither, and similarly those coming from Russia and northern territories who wish to cross to Turkey. The latter bring squirrel and ermine and other valuable furs, while the former carry materials of cotton or bombax, silk stuffs and sweet-smelling spices. To the east of this province is a city called Matrica [Taman]; here the river Tanais [Don] empties itself into the Sea of Pontus [Black Sea] through an opening twelve miles wide.

Before this river reaches the Sea of Pontus it forms a kind of sea [Sea of Azov] towards the north, which is seven hundred miles in breadth and length and nowhere reaches a depth of more than six paces; consequently large vessels do not enter it, but merchants from Constantinople going to the aforesaid city of Matrica send their barks as far as the river Tanais in order to buy dried fish, namely sturgeon and bar- bot and other fish in enormous quantities.

The said province of Cassaria is therefore girt on three sides by the sea, namely on the west where lies Kersona the city of Clement; on the south where is the city of Soldaia towards which we were steering and which forms the apex of the province, and on the east by the Sea of Tanais where the city of Matrica is and the outlet of the Sea of Tanais.

Beyond the mouth is Ziquia which is not subject to the Tartars, and to the east are the Suevi and Iberi [Georgians], who also do not obey them. Then towards the south is Trebizond which has its own ruler, by name Guido, who is of the stock of the Emperor of Constantinople and is subject to the Tartars. Next comes Sinopolis which belongs to the Sultan of Turkey who is likewise subject. Then there is the territory of Vastasius whose son is called Ascar after his maternal grandfather; he is not subject to them. From the mouth of the Tanais westwards as far as the Danube all is theirs, even beyond the Danube in the direction of Constantinople—Blakia which is the land of the Assans, Lesser Bulgaria even as far as Sclavonia, all pay them tribute: also in addition to the agreed tribute they have, in recent years, taken from each house one axe and all the unwrought iron which they found.

And so we reached Soldaia on May 21st. Certain merchants from Constantinople had arrived before us and had announced that envoys were coming thither from the Holy Land who wished to visit Sartach. Now I had preached publicly on Palm Sunday in St. Sophia's that I was not an envoy either of you or anybody else, but that I was going among these unbelievers in accordance with our Rule. Then when we landed the said merchants warned me to mind my words, for they had given out that I was an envoy, and if I were to deny that I was such, then I would not be allowed to proceed.

Thereupon I spoke in the following manner to the prefects of the city or rather to their deputies, for the prefects had gone to Baatu in the winter bearing their tribute and had not yet returned. "We heard it told of your lord Sartach in the Holy Land that he was a Christian and the Christians rejoiced exceedingly over this fact, espe- cially the most Christian lord, the King of the French, who is on a pilgrimage there and is fighting against the Saracens in order to wrest the Holy Places from their hands: for this reason I desire to go to Sartach and bring to him a letter of my lord the King, in which he admonishes him concerning the good estate of the whole of Christendom." They received us with joy and lodged us in the episcopal church. The Bishop of that church had been to Sartach and he told me many good things about him which I, for my part, was not to discover later.

They then gave us the choice as to whether we would like carts with oxen, or pack horses, to carry our belongings. The merchants from Constantinople advised us to accept the carts and even to buy covered carts for ourselves like the ones the Ruthenians use for carrying their furs, and into these to put such of our things as I did not wish to unpack every day; for if I took the horses, I should have to unload them at every stopping place and pack them on to other horses; moreover I would be able to ride at a more gentle pace with the oxen. I followed their advice, but it was bad advice for I was on the road for two months before I reached Sartach: a journey I could have completed in one month if I had gone with horses.

On the advice of the merchants I had brought with me from Constantinople fruit, muscatel wine and choice biscuits to present to the chief men of the city so that I might be granted permission to travel about, since they look with no favourable eye upon anyone coming to them empty-handed. On failing to find the prefects of the city there, I placed all these things in a cart, as I was told that Sartach would be delighted with them, if only I could get them as far as him.

So we set off on our journey about June 1st with our own four covered carts and with two others I had received from them in which was carried bedding for sleeping on at night. They gave us five horses to ride on, for we were five in number, myself, my companion Friar Bartholomew of Cremona, Gosset the bearer of this letter, Abdullah the interpreter, and a boy, Nicholas, whom I had bought at Constantinople out of the alms you gave me. They also gave us two men who drove the carts and looked after the oxen and horses.

There are lofty promontories along by the sea from Kersona as far as the mouth of the Tanais, and between Kersona and Soldaia there are forty small towns, practically each one of them having its own dialect; among them were many Goths who speak German.

Beyond these mountains towards the north is a most fair forest in a plain watered by springs and streams; on the other side of the forest is a vast plain which stretches northwards five days' journey to the boundary of this province where, having the sea to the east and west, it narrows so that there is a great dyke from one sea to the other. Before the Tartars came the Comans used to dwell in this plain and they obliged the aforementioned cities and fortresses to render them tribute; when the Tartars came the Comans entered this province, all fleeing as far as the sea-shore in such vast numbers that they ate each other, the living those who died, so I was told by a merchant who saw the living devouring and tearing with their teeth the raw flesh of the dead as dogs do corpses.

At the far end of this province are many large lakes, on the shores of which are salt-water springs; as soon as the water from these runs into the lake it turns into salt, hard like ice. Baatu and Sartach draw large revenues from these salt springs, for men come thither from the whole of Russia for salt, and for every cart-load they give two lengths of cotton valued at half an *yperpera*. Many ships also come by sea for the salt, all giving payment according to the amount each takes.

And so on the third day after leaving Soldaia we came across the Tartars; when I came among them it seemed indeed to me as if I were stepping into some other world, the life and customs of which I will describe for you as well as I can.

Chapter II

The Tartars and Their Dwellings

The Tartars have no abiding city nor do they know of the one that is to come. They have divided among themselves Scythia, which stretches from the Danube as far as the rising of the sun. Each captain, according to whether he has more or fewer men under him, knows the limits of his pasturage and where to feed his flocks in winter, summer, spring and autumn, for in winter they come down to the warmer districts in the south, in summer they go up to the cooler ones in the north. They drive their cattle to graze on the pasture lands without water in winter when there is snow there, for the snow provides them with water.

The dwelling in which they sleep has as its base a circle of interlaced sticks, and it is made of the same material; these sticks converge into a little circle at the top and from this a neck juts up like a chimney; they cover it with white felt and quite often they also coat the felt with lime or white clay and powdered bone to make it a more gleaming white, and sometimes they make it black. The felt round the neck at the top they decorate with lovely and varied paintings. Before the doorway they also hang felt worked in mulitcoloured designs; they sew coloured felt on to the other, making vines and trees, birds and animals. They make these houses so large that sometimes they are thirty feet across; for I myself once measured the width between the wheel tracks of a cart, and it was twenty feet, and when the house was on the cart it stuck out at least five feet beyond the wheels on each side. I have counted to one cart twenty-two oxen drawing one house, eleven in a row across the width of the cart, and the other eleven in front of them. The axle of the cart was as big as the mast of a ship, and a man stood at the door of the house on the cart, driving the oxen.

In addition they make squares to the size of a larger coffer out of slender split twigs; then over it, from one end to the other, they build up a rounded roof out of similar twigs and they make a little entrance at the front end; after that they cover this box or little house with black felt soaked in tallow or ewe's milk so that it is rain-proof, and this they decorate in the same way with multicoloured handwork. Into these chests they put all their bedding and valuables; they bind them onto high carts which are drawn by camels so that they can cross the rivers. These chests are never removed from the carts. When they take down their dwelling houses, they always put the door facing the south; then afterwards they draw up the carts with the chests on each side, half a stone's throw from the house, so that it stands between two rows of carts, as it were between two walls.

The married women make for themselves really beautiful carts which I would not know how to describe for you except by a picture; in fact I would have done you paintings of everything if I only knew how to paint. A wealthy Mongol or Tartar may well have a hundred or two hundred such carts with chests. Baatu has twenty-six wives and each of these has a large house, not counting the other small ones which are placed behind the large one and which are, as it were. chambers in which their attendants live; belonging to each of these houses are a good two hundred carts. When they pitch their houses the chief wife places her dwelling at the extreme west end and after her the others according to their rank, so that the last wife will be at the far east end, and there will be the space of a stone's throw between the establishment of one wife and that of another. And so the orda of a rich Mongol will look like a large town and yet there will be very few men in it.

One woman will drive twenty or thirty carts, for the country is flat. They tie together the carts, which are drawn by oxen or camels, one after the other, and the woman will sit on the front one driving the ox while all the others follow in step. If they happen to come on a bad bit of track they loose them and lead them across it one by one. They go at a very slow pace, as a sheep or an ox might walk.

When they have pitched their houses with the door facing south, they arrange the master's couch at the northern end. The women's place is always on the east side, that is, on the left of the master of the house when he is sitting on his couch looking towards the south; the men's place is on the west side, that is, to his right.

On entering a house the men would by no means hang up their quiver in the women's section. Over the head of the master there is always an idol like a doll or little image of felt which they call the master's brother, and a similar one over the head of the mistress, and this they call the mistress's brother; they are fastened on to the wall. Higher up between these two is a thin little one which is , as it were, the guardian of the whole house. The mistress of the house places on her right side, at the foot of the couch, in a prominent position, a goat-skin stuffed with wool or other material, and next to it a tiny image turned towards her attendants and the women. By the entrance on the women's side is still another idol with a cow's udder for the women who milk the cows, for this is the women's job. On the other side of the door towards the men is another image with a mare's udder for the men who milk the mares.

When they have foregathered for a drink they first sprinkle with the drink the idol over the master's head, then all the other idols in turn; after this an attendant goes out of the house with a cup and some drinks; he sprinkles thrice towards the south, genuflecting each time; this is in honour of fire; next towards the east in honour of the air, and after that to the west in honour of water; they cast it to the north for the dead. When the master is holding his cup in his hand and is about to drink, before he does so he first pours some out on the earth as its share. If he drinks while seated on a horse, before he drinks he pours some over the neck or mane of the horse. And so when the attendant has sprinkled towards the four quarters of the earth he returns into the house; two servants with two cups and as many plates are ready to carry the drink to the master and the wife sitting beside him upon his couch. If he has several wives, she with whom he sleeps at night sits next to him during the day, and on that day all the others have to come to her dwelling to drink, and the court is held there, and the gifts which are presented to the master are placed in the treasury of that wife. Standing in the entrance is a bench with a skin of milk or some other drink and some cups.

In the winter they make an excellent drink from rice, millet, wheat and honey, which is clear like wine. Wine, too, is conveyed to them from distant regions. In the summer they do not bother about anything except cosmos. Cosmos [kourniss] is always to be found inside the house before the entrance door, and near it stands a musician with his instrument. Our lutes and viols I did not see there but many other instruments such as are not known among us. When the master begins to drink, then one of the attendants cries out in a loud voice "Ha!" and the musician strikes his instrument. And when it is a big feast they are holding, they all clap their hands and also dance to the sound of the instrument, the men before the master and the women before the mistress. After the master has drunk, then the attendant cries out as before and the instrument-player breaks off. Then they drink all round, the men and the women, and sometimes vie with each other in drinking in a really disgusting and gluttonous manner.

When they want to incite anyone to drink they seize him by the ears and pull them vigorously to make his gullet open, and they clap and dance in front of him. Likewise when they want to make a great feast and entertainment for anyone, one man takes a full cup and two others stand, one on his right and one on his left, and in this manner the three, singing and dancing, advance right up to him to whom they are to offer the cup, and they sing and dance before him; when he stretches out his hand to take the cup they suddenly leap back, and then they advance again as before; and in this way they make fun of him, drawing back the cup three or four times until he is in a really lively mood and wants it: then they give him the cup and sing and clap, their hands and stamp with their feet while he drinks.

Chapter III

The Food of the Tartars

As for their food and victuals I must tell you they eat all dead animals indiscriminately and with so many flocks and herds you can be sure a great many animals do die. However, in the summer as long as they have any cosmos, that is mare's milk, they do not care about any other food. If during that time an ox or a horse happens to die they dry the flesh by cutting it into thin strips and hanging it in the sun and the wind, and it dries immediately without salt and without any unpleasant smell. Out of the intestines of horses they make sausages which are better than pork sausages and they eat these fresh; the rest of the meat they keep for the winter. From the hide of oxen they make large jars which they dry in a wonderful way in the smoke. From the hind part of horses' hide they make very nice shoes.

They feed fifty or a hundred men with the flesh of a single sheep, for they cut it up in little bits in a dish with salt and water, making no other sauce; then with the point of a knife or a fork especially made for this purpose—like those with which we are accustomed to eat pears and apples cooked in wine—they offer to each of those standing round one or two mouthfuls, according to the number of guests. Before the flesh of the sheep is served, the master first takes what pleases him; and also if he gives anyone a special portion then the one receiving it has to eat it himself and may give it to no one else. But if he cannot eat it all he may take it away with him or give it to his servant, if he is there, to keep for him; otherwise he may put it away in his *captargac*, that is, a square bag which they carry to put all such things in: in this they also keep bones when they have not the time to give them a good gnaw, so that later they may gnaw them and no food be wasted.

Chapter IV

How They Make Cosmos

Cosmos, that is mare's milk, is made in this way: they stretch along the ground a long rope attached to two stakes stuck into the earth, and at about nine o'clock they tie to this rope the foals of the mares they want to milk. Then the mothers stand near their foals and let themselves be peacefully milked; if any one of them is too restless, then a man takes the foal and, placing it under her, lets it suck a little, and he takes it away again and the milker takes its place.

And so, when they have collected a great quantity of milk, which is as sweet as cow's milk when it is fresh, they pour it into a large skin or bag and they begin churning it with a specially made stick which is as big as a man's head at its lower end, and hollowed out; and when they beat it quickly it begins to bubble like new wine and to turn sour and ferment, and they churn it until they can extract the butter. Then they taste it and when it is fairly pungent they drink it. As long as one is drinking, It bites the tongue like vinegar; when one stops, it leaves on the tongue the taste of milk of almonds and greatly delights the inner man; it even intoxicates those who have not a very good head. It also greatly provokes urine.

For use of the great lords they also make caracosmos, that is black cosmos, in this wise. Mare's milk does not curdle. Now it is a general rule that the milk of any animal, in the stomach of whose young rennet is not found, does not curdle; it is not found in the stomach of a young horse, hence the milk of a mare doest not curdle. And so they churn the milk until everything that is solid in it sinks right to the bottom like the lees of wine, and what is pure remains on top and is like whey or white must. The dregs are very white and are given to the slaves and have a most soporific effect. The clear liquid the masters drink and it is certainly a very pleasant drink and really potent.

Baatu has thirty men within a day's journey of his camp, each one of whom provides him every day with such milk from a hundred mares—that is to say, the milk of three thousand mares every day, not counting the other white milk which other men bring. For, just as in Syria the peasants give a third part of their produce, so these men have to bring to the orda of their lords the mare's milk of every third day.

From cow's milk they first extract the butter and this they boil until it is completely boiled down; then they store it in sheep's paunches which they keep for this purpose; they do not put salt into the butter; however it does not go bad owing to the long boiling. They keep it against the winter. The rest of the milk which is left after the butter has been extracted they allow to turn until it is as sour as it can be, and they boil it, and in boiling, it curdles; they dry the curd in the sun and it becomes as hard as iron slag, and this they keep in bags against the winter. During the winter months when there is a scarcity of milk, they put this sour curd, which they call *grut*, into a skin and pour hot water on top of it and beat it vigorously until it melts in the water, which, as a result, becomes completely sour, and this water they drink instead of milk. They take the greatest care never to drink plain water.

Chapter V

The Animals They Eat, Their Clothes and Their Hunting

The great lords have villages in the south from which millet and flour are brought to them for the winter; the poor provide for themselves by trading sheep and skins; and the slaves fill their bellies with dirty water and are content with this. They also catch mice, of which many kinds abound there; mice with long tails they do not eat but give to their birds; they eat dormice and all kinds of mice with short tails. There are also many marmots there which they call *sogur* and these congregate in one burrow in the winter, twenty or thirty of them together, and they sleep for six months; these they catch in great quantities.

Also to be found there are conies with a long tail like a cat and having at the tip of the tail black and white hairs. They have many other little animals as well which are good to eat, and they are very clever at knowing the difference. I saw no deer there, I saw few hares, many gazelles; wild asses I saw in great quantities and these are like mules. I also saw another kind of animal which is called *areali* and which has a body just like a ram's and horns twisted like a ram's but of such a size that I could scarce lift the two horns with one hand; and they make large cups out of these horns.

They have hawks, gerfalcons and peregrine falcons in great numbers and these they carry on their right hand, and they always put a little thong round the hawk's neck. This thong hangs down the middle of its breast and by it they pull down with the left hand the head and breast of the hawk when they cast it at its prey, so that it is not beaten back by the wind or carried upwards. They procure a large part of their food by the chase.

When they want to hunt wild animals they gather together in a great crowd and surround the district in which they know the animals to be, and gradually they close in until between them they shut in the animals in a circle and then they shoot at them with their arrows.

I will tell you about their garments and their clothing. From Cathay and other countries to the east, and also from Persia and other districts of the south, come cloths of silk and gold and cotton materials which they wear in the summer. From Russia, Moxel, Great Bulgaria and Pascatu, which is Greater Hungary, and Kerkis, which are all districts towards the north, and full of forests, and from many other regions in the north which are subject to them, valuable furs of many kinds are brought for them, such as I have never seen in our part of the world; and these they wear in winter. In the winter they always make at least two fur garments, one with the fur against the body, the other with the fur outside to the wind and snow, and these are usually of the skins of wolves or foxes or monkeys, and when they are sitting in their dwelling they have another softer one. The poor make their outer ones of dog and goat.

They also make trousers out of skins. Moreover, the rich line their garments with silk stuffing which is extraordinarily soft and light and warm. The poor line their clothes with cotton material and with the softer wool which they are able to pick out from the coarser. With the coarse they make felt to cover their dwellings and coffers and also for making bedding. Also with wool mixed with a third part horse-hair they make their ropes. From felt they make saddle pads, saddle cloths and rain cloaks, which means they use a great deal of wool. You have seen the men's costume.

Chapter VI

How the Men Shave and the Women Adorn Themselves

The men shave a square on the top of their heads and from the front corners of this they continue the shaving in strips along the sides of the head as far as the temples. They also shave their temples and neck to the top of the cervical cavity and their forehead in front to the top of the frontal bone, where they leave a tuft of hair which hangs down as far as the eyebrows. At the sides and the back of the head they leave the hair, which they make into plaits, and these they braid round the head to the ears.

The costume of the girls is no different from that of the men except that it is somewhat longer. But on the day after she is married a woman shaves from the middle of her head to her forehead, and she has a tunic as wide as a nun's cowl, and in every respect wider and longer, and open in front, and this they tie on the right side. Now in this matter the Tartars differ from the Turks, for the Turks tie their tunics on the left, but the Tartars always on the right.

They also have a head-dress which they call *bocca*, which is made out of the bark of a tree or of any other fairly light material which they can find; it is large and circular and as big as two hands can span around, a cubit and more high and square at the top like the capital of a column. This *bocca* they cover with costly silk material, and it is hollow inside, and on the capital in the middle or on the side they put a rod of quills or slender canes, likewise a cubit and more in length; and they decorate this rod at the top with peacock feathers and throughout its length all round with little feathers from the mallard's tail and also with precious stones. The wealthy ladies wear such an ornament on the top of their head and fasten it down firmly with a hood which has a hole in the top for this purpose, and in it they stuff their hair, gathering it up from the back on to the top of the head in a kind of knot and putting over it the *bocca* which they then tie firmly under the chin. So when several ladies ride together and are seen from a distance, they give the appearance of soldiers with helmets on their heads and raised lances; for the *bocca* looks like a helmet and the rod on top like a lance.

All the women sit on their horses like men, astride, and they tie their cowls with a piece of sky-blue silk round the waist, and with another strip they bind their breasts, and they fasten a piece of white stuff below their eyes which hangs down to the breast.

The women are wondrous fat and the less nose they have more beautiful they are considered. They disfigure themselves hideously by painting their faces. They never lie down on a bed to give birth to their children.

Chapter VII

The Duties of the Women and Their Work

It is the duty of the women to drive the carts, to load the houses on to them and to unload them, to milk the cows, to make the butter and *grut*, to dress the skins and to sew them, which they do with thread made out of tendons. They split the tendons into very thin threads and then twist these into one long thread. They also sew shoes and socks and other garments. They never wash their clothes, for they say that that makes God angry and that it would thunder if they hung them out to dry; they even beat those who do wash them and take them away from them. They are extraordinarily afraid of thunder. At such a time they turn all strangers out of their dwellings and wrap themselves in black felt in which they hide until it has passed over. They never wash their dishes, but when the meat is cooked, they wash out the bowl in which they are going to put it with some boiling broth from the cauldron which they afterwards pour back. The women also make the felt and cover the houses

The men make bows and arrows, manufacture stirrups and bits and make saddles; they build the houses and carts, they look after the horses and milk the mares, churn the cosmos, that is the mares' milk, and make the skins in which it is kept, and they also look after the camels and load them. Both sexes look after the sheep and goats, and sometimes the men, sometimes the women, milk them. They dress skins with sour milk of ewes, thickened and salted.

When they want to wash their hands or their head, they fill their mouth with water and, pouring this little by little from their mouth into their hands, with it they wet their hair and wash their head.

As for their marriages, you must know that no one there has a wife unless he buys her, which means that sometimes girls are quite grown up before they marry, for their parents always keep them until they sell them. They observe the first and second degrees of consanguinity, but observe no degrees of affinity; they have two sisters at the same time or one after the other. No widow among them marries, the reason being that they believe that all those who serve them in this life will serve them in the next, and so of a widow they believe that she will always return after death to her first husband. This gives rise to a shameful custom among them whereby a son sometimes takes to wife all his father's wives, except his own mother; for the order of a father and mother always falls to the youngest son and so he himself has to provide for all his father's wives who come to him with his father's effects; and then, if he so wishes, he uses them as wives, for he does not consider an injury has been done to him if they return to his father after death.

And so when anyone has made an agreement with another to take his daughter, the father of the girl arranges a feast and she takes flight to relations where she lies hid. Then the father declares: "Now my daughter is yours; take her wherever you find her." Then he searches for her with his friends until he finds her; then he has to take her by force and bring her, as though by violence, to his house.

Chapter VIII
Of Their Justice and Judgments, Death and Burial

Concerning their penal laws I can tell you that when two men fight no one dares to interfere, even a father dare not help his son, but he who comes off the worse may appeal to the court of the lord and if the other touches him after the appeal, he is put to death. But he must go immediately without any delay and the one who has suffered the injury leads the other like a captive.

They inflict capital punishment on no one unless he has been caught in the act or confesses; but when a man is accused by a number of people, they torture him well, so that he confesses. Murder they punish by the death sentence, and also cohabiting with a woman not one's own. By one's own I mean wife or servant, for it is lawful for a man to use his slave as he will. Robbery on a grand scale they likewise punish by death. For a petty theft, such as one sheep, so long as a man has not been caught doing it often, they beat him cruelly, and if they deal him a hundred strokes, then they have to have a hundred rods. I am speaking of those who are beaten as a result of the court's sentence. Similarly they put to death false ambassadors, that is to say men who pretend they are ambassadors but are not; also sorceresses, of whom however I will tell you more later, for they consider them to be witches.

When anyone dies they mourn, wailing in a loud voice, and then they are free from paying taxes until the year is up. And if anyone is present at the death of an adult, he does not enter the dwelling of Mangu Chan for a year; if it is a child who dies he does not enter it for a month.

Near the grave of a dead man they always leave a dwelling, if he is of the nobility, that is of the family of Chingis, who was their first father and lord. The burial place of him who dies is not known; and always around those places where they bury their nobles there is a camp of men who guard the tombs. It has not come to my knowledge that they bury treasure with the dead. The Comans make a great mound over the dead man and set up a statue to him, facing the east and holding a cup in its hand in front of its navel. They also make pyramids for the rich, that is, little pointed houses; and in some places I saw large towers of baked tiles, and in others stone houses, although stones are not to be found there. I saw a man recently dead for whom they had hung up, between tall poles, the skins of sixteen horses, four facing each quarter of the earth, and they had put cosmos there for him to drink and meat for him to eat, and in spite of this they said of him that he had been baptised. Further east I saw other tombs, namely large areas strewn with stones, some round, some square and then four tall stones upright round the plot facing the four quarters of the earth.

When anyone is ill he takes to his bed and places a sign above his dwelling that there is a sick person there and that no one may enter. And so nobody visits the invalid except the one who looks after him. When anyone from one of the great ordas is sick, they place guards at a distance round the orda and they do not allow anyone to cross these bounds, for they are afraid an evil spirit of wind may come in with those entering. They summon their soothsayers as if they were their priests.

Chapter XXXVI

Of the Chan's Festivals, the Letter To Be Sent to King Louis and Friar William's Return

After the feast of Pentecost they began to compose the letter which the Chan was to send to you. In the meantime he returned to Caracorum and held his great reception just on the octave of Pentecost, and he wanted all the envoys to be present on the last day. He also sent for us but I had gone to the church to baptize the three children of a poor German I had come across there. For that feast Master William was the chief cup-bearer because he had made the tree which pours forth drink; and all, rich and poor, sang and danced and clapped their hands in front of the Chan. He then began to address them, saying: "I have parted with my brothers and have sent them into danger against foreign nations. Now we shall see what you will do when I wish to send you to extend our empire." On each of the four days they changed their clothes, which they gave to them on each day all of one colour, from the shoes to the headdress.

At that time I saw the envoy of the Caliph of Baghdad there; he had himself conveyed to the court in a litter between two mules, which led some to say that the Chan had made peace with them, the condition being that they should provide him with an army of ten thousand horsemen. Others were saying that Mangu had declared he would not make peace with them unless they destroyed all their fortifications, and the envoy had replied: " When you take all the hooves off your horses, we will destroy all our fortifications."

I also saw there the envoys of a Sultan of India who had brought eight leopards and ten greyhounds trained to sit on the back of a horse like leopards. When I asked about India, in what direction it was from that spot, they pointed towards the west, and the envoys accompanied me on our return journey for about three weeks, traveling all the time westwards. I saw too, envoys of the Sultan of Turkey, who brought costly presents for the Chan; he replied, so I heard, that he had need of neither gold nor silver but of men; by this he meant he wanted them to provide him with an army.

On the feast of St. John [June 24th] the Chan held a great drinking festival and I counted a hundred and five carts laden with mares' milk, and ninety horses; and the same on the feast of the Apostles Peter and Paul [June 29th].

The letter he is sending to you being at length finished, I was summoned and they translated it. I have written down the gist of it as well as I could grasp it by means of an interpreter and it is as follows:

"This is the decree of the eternal God. In heaven there is but one eternal God, on earth there is but one lord Chingis Chan, the son of God, Demugin Cingei, that is the sound of iron." (They call Chingis the sound of iron because he was a smith; and puffed up with pride they now call him the son of God.)

"This is the message which is spoken to you: whosoever there be Mongol, or Naiman, or Merkit, or Mussulman, wherever ears can hear and whithersoever a horse can go, there make it heard and understood: from the time they hear my decree and understand, and will not to believe, but wish to make war against us, you will hear and will see that they will have eyes, but will not see, and when they wish to hold anything they will be without hands, and when they wish to walk they will be without feet. This is the decree of the eternal God. By the power of the eternal God throughout the great realm of the Mongols, let the decree of Mangu Chan be known to the lord of the Franks, King Louis and to all the other lords and priests and to all the world of the Franks so that they may understand our message. The decree of the eternal God was made by Chingis Chan, but this decree has not reached you from Chingis Chan or from others after him.

"A certain man, David by name, came to you as if he were an envoy of the Mongols but he was a liar, and you sent your envoys with him to Keu Chan. It was after the death of Keu Chan that your envoys arrived at his orda. Chamus his wife sent you cloths of *nasic* and a letter. But how could that wicked woman, more vile than a dog, know about matters of war and affairs of peace, and how to pacify a great race and see how to act for good?

(Mangu told me with his own lips that Chamus was the worst kind of witch and that by her sorcery she had destroyed her whole family.)

"The two monks, who came from you to Sartach, Sartach sent to Baatu; Baatu however, seeing that Mangu Chan is chief over the Mongol people, sent them to us.

"Now, in order that the great world and the priests an the monks might all live in peace and rejoice in the good things of life and in order that the decree of God might be heard among them, we wished to appoint Mongol envoys to accompany your aforementioned priests. The priests however gave answer that between us and you there was a land of war and many evil men and difficult going, and therefore they were afraid they would be unable to bring our envoys to you safe and sound, but they said that if we gave them our letter containing our decree they would take it to King Louis. This is the reason why we have not sent our envoys with them, but by the hands of these your priests we have sent to you the decree of the eternal God in writing.

"It is the decree of the eternal God which we have made known to you. When you have heard and believed it, if you wish to obey us, send your envoys to us; in this way we shall know for sure whether you wish to be at peace or war with us. When by the power of the eternal God the whole world from the rising of the sun to the going down thereof shall be at one in joy and peace, then it will be made clear what we are going to do; it, when you hear and understand the decree of the eternal God, you are unwilling to pay attention and believe it, saying 'Our country is far away, our mountains are mighty, our sea is vast', and in this confidence you bring an army against us—we know what we can do: He who made what was difficult easy and what was far away near, the eternal God, He knows."

At first they called us your envoys in this letter. Then I said to them, "Do not call us by the name of envoys, for I have told the Chan clearly that we are not envoys of King Louis." They went to him and told him; on their return they said he had taken it in good part and had ordered them to write what I should say to them. So I told them to remove the title of envoy and to call us monks or priests.

In the meantime, while this was being done, my companion heard that we were to return through the wilderness to Baatu and that a Mongol was to be our guide, so, unknown to me, he ran to Bulgai the chief scribe and intimated to him by means of signs that he would die if he were to go on that journey. When the day arrived on which we were to be given our leave to depart, that is to say a fortnight after the feast of St. John [July 9th or 10th], when we were summoned to the court, the scribes said to my companion: "See, Mangu wishes your companion to return by way of Baatu, and you say you are a sick man and it is clear that you are. Mangu therefore says, if you wish to go with your companion you may go, but on your own head be it, for perhaps you will stay at the house of some *yam*, and he will not make provision for you and you will be a hindrance to your companion; if, on the other hand, you wish to remain here, the Chan will provide you with what you need until some envoys arrive with whom you can make the return journey more slowly and by a route along which there are towns." The Friar replied: " God grant the Chan good fortune! I will remain." I however said to the Friar, "Brother, take heed to what you are doing. It is not I who am forsaking you." "You," said he, "are not forsaking me, but I am leaving you, for if I go with you, I shall see both my body and soul in danger, for I cannot endure such intolerable hardship."

The scribes were holding three garments or tunics and they said to us: "You do not wish to receive gold or silver and you have been here a long time praying for the Chan; he begs you at least to accept, each one of you, a simple tunic, so that you may not leave him empty-handed." We then had to accept them out of respect to him, for they take it ill when their gifts are disdained. He had frequently before sent to ask us what we wanted and we always gave the same answer, so much that the Christians there scoffed at the pagans, who look for nothing but presents. The pagans used to reply that we were fools, for if he wished to give them his whole orda, they would gladly accept it and they would be acting prudently. When we had received the garments they asked us to say a prayer for the Chan, which we did. And so having obtained our leave we went to Caracorum.

It happened on day while we were with the monk some distance away from the court along with the other envoys that the monk sounded the board so loudly, that Mangu Chan heard it and enquired what it was. They told him and he asked why the monk was so far removed from the orda. They explained that it was troublesome to bring him horses and oxen every day to the orda, and added that it would be better for him to stay at Caracorum near the church and pray there. Then the Chan sent to him saying that if he wished to go to Caracorum and stay there near the church he would give him all he needed. The monk however replied: "I came here from the Holy Land of Jerusalem by the command of God, and I left a city in which there are a thousand churches better than the one in Caracorum; if he wishes me to stay here and pray for him, as God commanded me, I will stay; otherwise I will go back to the place I came from." That evening oxen harnessed to carts were brought for him, and the following morning he was taken back to the site he used to occupy in front of the court.

Shortly before our departure a Nestorian monk arrived, who seemed a prudent man. Bulgai, the chief scribe, placed him before his own orda and the Chan sent his children to receive his blessing. And so we came to Caracorum, and while we were in Master William's house, my guide arrived bearing ten *iascot*, five of which he put into Master William's hand, saying that he was to spend them on behalf of the Chan for the needs of the Friar; the other five he placed in the hand of Abdullah, my interpreter, ordering him to spend them on the journey for my needs. Unknown to us Master William had put them up to this.

I immediately sold one of the *iascot* and distributed it among the poor Christians there who all looked to us for help; another we spent in purchasing necessary clothes and other things of which we stood in need; with the third Abdullah made some purchases by means of which he earned a little profit for himself. The rest we also spent there, for nowhere from the time we entered Persia were we given a sufficient supply of necessities, not even among the Tartars, and there we seldom came across anything for sale.

Master William, at one time your subject, sends you a leather strap ornamented with a precious stone which they carry as a protection against thunder and lightning, and he sends you countless greetings and prays for you; for him I could never render sufficient thanks to God or to you.

There we baptised in all six souls.

And so we parted from each other with tears, my companion remaining with Master William while I returned alone with my interpreter, with my guide and a servant who had an order that he would receive a sheep in four days' time for the four of us.

Study Questions

1. What is William's description of the dwelling or shelter of the "Tartars, " or Mongols?
2. What drinks did the Mongols have?
3. What was the Mongols' only food in summertime?
4. What was '"cosmos" [kumiss, airagh]? How was it made?
5. What did the Mongols never drink?
6. What was the Mongols' method of hunting wild animals?
7. Where did the Mongols get the materials for their clothes?
8. Of what were the Mongols extraordinarily afraid?
9. What did Mongolian men make?
10. What was the custom for a man to take a woman as his wife after he agreed with her family to do so?
11. What capital crimes did the Mongols have?
12. What was the thrust of the letter of Möngke ("Mangus") to King Louis?

13. Did William encounter any Christians along his travels?

14. How many people did they baptize?

G. Juvaini

The Persian Ala-ad-Din Ala-Malik Juvaini (1226–1283) was born in Khorasan (in modern Iran) the year before Genghis Khan died. He was destined to become the great historian of the rise of the Mongol world empire. He actually entered the Mongols' service and began his history in 1252 in Karakorum, a Mongolian city (really more of a semi-permanent guarded encampment) and the capital of the Mongol world empire.

Juvaini, a devout Muslim, obviously could not approve of all of the Mongols' actions, but he did see much good in them and attempted to discern divine justice and the hand of God in them. As a Muslim, he could only try to see God's will in the Mongol onslaught. He could hardly excoriate the Mongols in whose service he labored, but there are subtle hints in his writing that he preferred the Islamic past to the Mongol-dominated present. He did have genuine praise for Chinggis Khan and wrote that Alexander the Great could have been his pupil. He did see some good in the Mongolian invasions: they produced martyrs for Islam and introduced the religion into regions that had not previously known it. He approved heartily of the Mongols' defeat of the Assassins or Ismailis (a heretical Islamic sect) in Persia in the 1250s at the hands of the Mongols, and he personally burned the library of Ismaili books in Alamut, Persia after its capture by Mongol forces.

Juvaini accompanied the Mongols on their campaigns against Baghdad and the Abbasid Caliphate. The Mongols then appointed him governor over the city and other territories once directly ruled by the caliph, and he served in this capacity for twenty years. Juvaini wrote his history intermittently between 1252 and 1260, when he finally gave up on the work due to his preoccupation with politics and administrative matters.

Juvaini's work, *History of the World-Conqueror*, is incomplete. It contains errors, blanks he meant to fill in later, and references to non-existent chapters. His language in it is ornate, convoluted, and contains many allusions and plays on words. You should get some feel for his way with language even in the translated passages that follow below.

149

The History of the World-Conqueror

Ala-ad-Din Ata-Malik Juvaini

Of the Condition of the Mongols Before the Time of Chingiz-Khan's Rise to Power

When the phoenix (*humā*) of prosperity wishes to make the roof of one man its abode, and the owl of misfortune to haunt the threshold of another, though their stations be widely different, the one in the zenith of good fortune and the other in the nadir of abasement, yet neither scarcity of equipment nor feebleness of condition prevents the fortunate man from attaining his goal—

> Whoever hath been prepared for Fortune, though he seek her not,
> Fortune seeketh him—

and neither abundance of gear nor excess of accoutrement can save the unfortunate one from losing even that which he hath.

'*Exertion unaided by fortune is illusive.*' Nor may the counsel of man lay the hand of protection upon his brow; but '*when he prospereth, he prospereth, and when he faileth, he faileth*'. For if craft, and might, and wealth, and affluence could accomplish aught, then would power and empire never have passed from the houses of former kings to another; but when the time of the decline of their fortunes was arrived, neither craft, nor perseverance nor counsel could aid them; and neither the multitude of their troops nor the strength of their resistance was of any avail. And of this there is still clearer proof and plainer evidence in the instance of the Mongol people, when one considers in what circumstances and position they found themselves before they beat the drum of the greatness of Chingiz-Khan and his posterity, and how to-day the waters of prosperity flow in the rivers of their desire and the army of affliction and sorrow has fallen upon the stations and relays of opponents and insurgents, which same were mighty Chosroes and illustrious kings; and in what manner Fate has shown herself kind to that people, and how the world was stirred up by them, [15] prisoners becoming princes and princes prisoners. '*And that was easy unto God.*'

> Upon the head of a slave a crown of honour that adorneth him, and on the foot
> of a freeman a chain of shame that disfigureth him.

The home of the Tartars, and their origin and birthplace, is an immense valley, whose area is a journey of seven or eight months both in length and breadth. In the east it marches with the land of Khitai, in the west with the country of the Uighur, in the north with the Qirqiz and the river Selengei and in the south with the Tangut and the Tibetans.

Before the appearance of Chingiz-Khan they had no chief or ruler. Each tribe or two tribes lived separately; they were not united with one another, and there was constant fighting and hostility between them. Some of them regarded robbery and violence, immorality and debauchery (*fisq va fujūr*) as deeds of manliness and excellence. The Khan of Khitai used to demand and seize goods from them. Their clothing was of the skins of dogs and mice, and their food was the flesh of those animals and other dead things; their wine was mares' milk and their dessert the fruit of a tree shaped like the pine, which, they call *qusuq* and besides which no other fruit-bearing tree will grow in that region: it grows [even] on some of the mountains, where, on account of the excessive cold, there is nothing else to be found. The sign of a great emir amongst them was that his stirrups were of iron; from which one can form a picture of their other luxuries. And they continued in this indigence, privation and misfortune until the banner of Chingiz-Khan's fortune was raised and they issued forth from the straits of hardship into the amplitude of well-being, from a prison into a garden, from the desert of poverty into a palace of delight and from abiding torment into reposeful pleasances; their raiment being of silk and brocade, their food and fruit ' *The flesh of birds of the kind which they shall desire, and fruits of the sort which they shall choose,*' and their drink '*(pure wine) sealed; the seal whereof shall be musk.*' And so it has come to pass that the present world is the paradise of that people; for all the merchandise that is brought from the West is borne unto them, and that which is bound in the farthest East is untied in their houses; wallets and purses are filled from their treasuries, and their everyday garments are studded with jewels and embroidered with gold; and in the markets of their residences gems and fabrics have been so much cheapened [16] that were the former taken back to the mine or quarry they would sell there for more than double the price, while to take fabrics thither is as to bear a present of carraway-seeds to Kerman or an offering of water to Oman. Moreover, everyone of them has laid out fields and everywhere appointed husbandmen; their victuals, too, are abundant, and their beverages flow like the River Oxus.

Through the splenldour of the daily increasing fortune and under the shadow of the august majesty of Chingiz-Khan and his descendants the circumstances of the Mongols have risen from such penury and indigence to such abundance and affluence. And as for the other tribes their affairs also have been well ordered and their destiny firmly established. And whoever could not [previously] afford to make himself a cotton bed will trade with them for fifty thousand or thirty thousand gold or silver *balish* at a time. Now the *balish* is worth fifty *misqals* of gold or silver, round about seventy-five *rukni* dinars, the standard of which is two thirds.

May God Almighty grant his posterity, and in particular Mengü Qa'an, who is a most wise and just monarch, countless years in the pursuit of a prosperous life; may He uphold his clemency towards mankind!

The Capture of Bukhara

. . . In the Eastern countries Bukhara is the cupola of Islam and in those regions she is like unto the City of Peace [Baghdad]. Her environs are adorned with the brightness of the light of doctors and jurists and her surroundings embellished with the rarest of high attainments. Since ancient times she has in every age been the place of assembly of the great savants of every religion. Now the derivation of Bukhara is from *bukhār* [Vihāra], which in the language of the Magians [correctly: the Buddhists] signifies center of learning. . . .

Chinggiz Khan, having completed the organization and equipment of his armies, arrived in the countries of the Sultan [the Khwārizm-Shāh Muhammad II]; and dispatching his elder sons and the *noyans* in every direction at the head of large forces, he himself advanced first upon Bukhara, being accompanied by Toluy alone of his elder sons and by a host of fearless Turks that knew not clean from unclean, and considered the bowl of war to be a basin of rich soup and held a mouthful of the sword to be a beaker of wine.

He proceeded along the road to Zarnūq [near Otrār], and in the morning when the king of the planets raised his banner on the eastern horizon, he arrived unexpectedly before the town. When the inhabitants thereof, who were unaware of the fraudulent designs of Destiny, beheld the surrounding countryside choked with horsemen and the air black as night with the dust of cavalry, fright and panic overcame them, and fear and dread prevailed. They betook themselves to the citadel and closed the gates, thinking, 'This is perhaps a single detachment of a great army and a single wave from a raging sea.' It was their intention to resist and to approach calamity on their own feet, but they were aided by divine grace so that they stood firm and breathed not opposition. At this juncture, the World-Emperor, in accordance with his constant practice, dispatched Dānishmend Hājib upon an embassy to them, to announce the arrival of his forces and to advise them to stand out of the way of a dreadful deluge. Some of the inhabitants, who were in the category of 'Satan hath gotten mastery over them' [Koran 58:20], were minded to do him harm and mischief; whereupon he raised a shout, saying: 'I am such-and-such a person, a Muslim and the son of a Muslim. Seeking God's pleasure I am come on an embassy to you, at the inflexible command of Chinggiz Khan, to draw you out of the whirlpool of destruction and the trough of blood. It is Chinggiz Khan himself who has come with many thousands of warriors. The battle has reached thus far. If you are incited to resist in any way, in an hour's time your citadel will be level ground and the plain a sea of blood. But if you will listen to advice and exhortation with the ear of intelligence and consideration and become submissive and obedient to his command, your lives and property will remain in the stronghold of security.' When the people, both nobles and commoners, had heard his words, which bore the brand of veracity, they did not refuse to accept his advice, knowing for certain that the flood might not be stemmed by their obstructing his passage nor might the quaking of the mountains and the earth be quietened and allayed by the pressure of their feet. And so they held it proper to choose peace and advantageous to accept advice. But by way of caution and security they obtained from him a covenant that if, after the people had gone forth to meet the Khan and obeyed his command, any harm should befall any one of them, the retribution thereof should be on his head. Thus were the people's minds set at ease, and they withdrew their feet from the thought of transgression and turned their faces toward the path of advantage. The chief men of Zarnūq sent forward a delegation bearing presents. When these came to the place where the Emperor's cavalry had halted, he asked about their leaders and notables and was wroth with them for their dilatoriness in remaining behind. He dispatched a messenger to summon them to his presence. Because of the great awe in which the Emperor was held a tremor of horror appeared on the limbs of these people like the quaking of the members of a mountain. They at once proceeded to his presence; and when they arrived he treated them with mercy and clemency and spared their lives, so that they were once more of good heart. An order was then issued that everyone in Zarnūq—be he who he might—both such as donned *kulah* and turban and such as wore kerchief and veil, should go out of the town on to the plain. The citadel was turned into level ground; and after a counting of heads they made a levy of the youths and young men for the attack on Bukhara, while the rest of the people were suffered to return home. They gave the place the name of Qutlugh Bahgh [roughly 'Fortunate Town']. A guide, one of the Turcomans of that region, who had a perfect knowledge of the roads and highways, led them on by a little frequented road; which road has ever since been called the *Khan's Road*. . . .

Dayir Bahādur was proceeding in advance of the main forces. When he and his men drew near to the town of Nur Nūrata] they passed through some gardens. During the night they felled the trees and fashioned ladders out of them. Then holding the ladders in front of their horses they advanced very slowly: and the watcher on the walls thought that they were a caravan of merchants, until in this manner they arrived at the gates of the citadel of Nur; when the day of that people was darkened and their eyes dimmed. . . .

To be brief, the people of Nur closed their gates; and Dayir Bahādur sent an envoy to announce the arrival of the World-Conquering Emperor and to induce them to submit and cease resistance. The feelings of the inhabitants were conflicting, because they did not believe that the World-Conquering Emperor Chinggiz Khan had arrived in person, and on the other hand they were apprehensive about the Sultan [Khwārizm-Shāh]. They were therefore uncertain what course to take, some being in favor of submission and surrender while others were for resistance or were afraid [to take any action]. Finally, after much coming and going of ambassadors, it was agreed that the people of Nur should prepare an offering of food and send it to the Lord of the Age together with an envoy, and so declare their submission and seek refuge in servitude and obedience.

Dayir Bahādur gave his consent and was satisfied with only a small offering. He then went his own way; and the people of Nur dispatched an envoy in the manner that had been agreed upon. After the envoys [sic] had been honored with the Emperor's acceptance of their offering, he commanded that they should surrender the town to [the general] Sübödäi, who was approaching Nur with the vanguard. When Sübödäi arrived they complied with this command and delivered up the town. Hereupon an agreement was reached that the people of Nur should be content with the deliverance of the community from danger and the retention of what was absolutely necessary for their livelihood and the pursuit of husbandry and agriculture, such as sheep and cows; and that they should go out on to the plain leaving their houses exactly as they were so that they might be looted by the army. They executed this order, and the army entered the town and bore off whatever they found there. The Mongols abided by this agreement and did no harm to any of them. The people of Nur then selected sixty men and dispatched them, together with Il-Khoja, the son of the Emir of Nur, to Dabus to render assistance to the Mongols. When Chinggiz Khan arrived, they went forth to meet him bearing suitable [presents] in the way of *tuzghu* and offerings of food. Chinggiz Khan distinguished them with royal favor and asked them what fixed taxes the Sultan drew from Nur. They replied that these amounted to 1500 dinars; and he commanded them to pay this sum in cash and they should suffer no further inconvenience. Half of this amount was produced from the women's ear-rings, and they gave security for the rest and [finally] paid it to the Mongols. And so were the people of Nur delivered from the humiliation of Tatar bondage and slavery, and Nur regained its splendor and prosperity.

And from thence Chinggiz Khan proceeded to Bukhara, and in the beginning of Muharram, 617 [March 1220], he encamped before the gates of the citadel. . . . And his troops were more numerous than ants or locusts, being in their multitude beyond estimation or computation. Detachment after detachment arrived, each like a billowing sea, and encamped round about the town. At sunrise twenty thousand men from the Sultan's auxiliary army (*bīrunī*) issued forth from the citadel together with most of the inhabitants; being commanded by Gök Khan and other officers. . . . Gök Khan was said to be a Mongol and to have fled from Chinggiz Khan and joined the Sultan; . . . as a consequence of which his affairs had greatly prospered. When these forces reached the banks of the Oxus [now Amu Darya], the patrols and advance parties of the Mongol army fell upon them and left no trace of them. . . .

On the following day when from the reflection of the sun the plain seemed to be a tray filled with blood, the people of Bukhara opened their gates and closed the door of strife and battle. The *imāms* [priests] and notables came on a deputation to Chinggiz Khan, who entered to inspect the town and the citadel. He rode into the Friday mosque and pulled up before the *maqsūra* [place of the priest in prayer], whereupon his son Toluy dismounted and ascended the pulpit. Chinggiz Khan asked those present whether this was the palace of the Sultan; they replied that it was the house of God. Then he too got down from his horse, and mounting two or three steps of the pulpit he exclaimed: 'The countryside is empty of fodder; fill our horses' bellies.' Whereupon they opened all the magazines in the town and began carrying off the grain. And they [the Mongols] brought the cases in which the Korans were kept out into the courtyard of the mosque, where they cast the Korans right and left and turned the cases into mangers for their horses. After which they circulated cups of wine and sent for the singing-girls of the town to sing and dance for them; while the Mongols raised their voices to the tunes of their own songs. Meanwhile, the *imāms, shaikhs, sayyids*, doctors and scholars of the age kept watch over their horses in the stable under the supervision of the equerries, and executed their commands. After an hour or two Chinggiz Khan arose to return to his camp, and as the multitude that had been gathered there moved away the leaves of the Koran were trampled in the dirt beneath their own feet and their horses' hoofs. In that moment, the Emir Imām Jalāl ad-Dīn Ali b. al-Hasan Zaidī who was the chief and leader of the *sayyids* of Transoxiana and was famous for his piety and asceticism, turned to the learned *imām* Rukn-ad-Dīn Imāmzmāda, who was one of the most excellent savants in the world . . ., and said: 'Maulānā, what state is this? *That which I see do I see it in wakefulness or in sleep, O Lord?*' Maulānā Imāmzmāda answered: 'Be silent: it is the wind of God's omnipotence that bloweth, and we have no power to speak.'

When Chinggiz Khan left the town he went to the festival *musallà* and mounted the pulpit; and, the people having been assembled, he asked which were the wealthy amongst them. Two hundred and eighty persons were designated (a hundred and ninety of them being natives of the town and the rest strangers, viz. ninety merchants from various places) and were led before him. He then began a speech, in which, after describing the resistance and treachery of the Sultan . . ., he addressed them as follows: 'O people, know that you have committed great sins, and that the great ones among you have committed these sins. If you ask me what proof I have for these words, I say it is because I am the punishment of God. If you had not committed great sins, God would not have sent a punishment like me upon you.' When he had finished speaking in this strain, he continued his discourse with words of admonition, saying, 'There is no need to declare your property that is on the face of the earth; tell me of that which is in the belly of the earth.' Then he asked them who were their men of authority; and each man indicated his own people. To each of them he assigned a Mongol or Turk as *basqaq* [tax collector] in order that the soldiers might not molest them, and, although not subjecting them to disgrace or humiliation, they began to exact money from these men; and when they delivered it up they did not torment them by excessive punishment or demanding what was beyond their power to pay. And every day, at the rising of the greater luminary, the guards would bring a party of notables to the audience-hall of the World-Emperor.

Chinggiz Khan had given orders for the Sultan's troops to be driven out of the interior of the town and the citadel. As it was impossible to accomplish this purpose by employing the townspeople and as these troops, being in fear of their lives, were fighting, and doing battle, and making night attacks as much as was possible, he now gave orders for all the quarters of the town to be set on fire; and since the houses were built entirely of wood, within several days the greater part of the town had been consumed, with the exception of the Friday mosque and some of the palaces, which were built with baked bricks. Then the people of Bukhara were driven against the citadel. And on either side the furnace of battle was heated. On the outside, mangonels were erected, bows bent and stones and arrows discharged; and on the inside, ballistas and pots of naphtha were set in motion. It was like a red-hot furnace fed from without by hard sticks thrust into the recesses, while from the belly of the furnace sparks shot into the air. For days they fought in this manner; the garrison made sallies against the besiegers, and Gök Khan in particular, who in bravery would have borne the palm from male lions, engaged in many battles; in each attack he overthrew several persons and alone repelled a great army. But finally they were reduced to the last extremity; resistance was no longer in their power; and they stood excused before God and man. The moat had been filled with animate and inanimate and raised up with levies and Bukharians; the outworks had been captured and fire hurled into the citadel; and their khans, leaders and notables, who were the chief men of the age and the favorites of the Sultan and who in their glory would set their feet on the head of Heaven, now became the captives of abasement and were drowned in the sea of annihilation. . . . Of the Qangli no male was spared who stood higher than the butt of a whip and more than thirty thousand were counted amongst the slain; whilst their small children, the children of their nobles and their womenfolk, slender as the cypress, were reduced to slavery.

When the town and the citadel had been purged of rebels and the walls and outworks levelled with the dust, all the inhabitants of the town, men and women, ugly and beautiful, were driven out on to the field of the *musallà* (summer mosque). Chinggiz Khan spared their lives; but the youths and full-grown men that were fit for such service were pressed into a levy (*hashar*) for the attack on Samarkand and Dābūsīya. Chinggiz Khan then proceeded against Samarkand and the people of Bukhara, because of the desolation, were scattered like the constellation of the Bear and departed into the villages, while the site of the town became like '*a level plain*'.

Now one man had escaped from Bukhara after its capture and had come to Khurasan. He was questioned about the fate of that city and replied: 'They came, they sapped, they burnt, they slew, they plundered and they departed.' Men of understanding who heard this description were all agreed that in the Persian language there could be nothing more concise than this speech. And indeed all that has been written in this chapter is summed up and epitomized in these two or three words.

. . . Finally, when, by the order of the World-Emperor [Ögädäi, 1229–41] . . ., the keys of government were placed in the solicitous hands of the Minister Yalavach, those scattered and dispersed in nooks and crannies were by the magnet of his justice and clemency attracted back to their former homes, and from all parts of the world people turned their faces thitherward; for because of his solicitude the prosperity of the town was on the increase, nay it reached its highest pitch and its territory became the home of the great and noble and the place of assembly of patrician and plebeian.

Suddenly in the year 636/1238–39 a sieve-maker of Tārāb in the district of Bukhara rose up in rebellion in the dress of the people of rags [mystics], and the common people rallied to his standard; and finally things came to such a pass that [after the rebellion had been stamped out] orders were given for the execution of all the inhabitants of Bukhara. But the Minister Yalavach, like a good prayer, averted their evil fate and by his mercy and solicitude repelled from them this sudden calamity. . . . And day by day the bounty of God's favor, by dint of which mercy and compassion everywhere form the carpet of justice and munificence, shines forth like the sun in the mercy of Mahmūd (=Yalavach) and the pearl of that sea, namely Mas'ud [his son and successor]. . . .

(Juvaini, *History of the World-Conqueror*, trans. Boyle, I, 97–108 [=Part I, 75–84].)

Study Questions

1. According to Juvaini, what was the condition of the Tartars prior to the appearance of Chingiz-Khan (Chinggis Khan, Genghis Khan)?

2. Before Chinggis Khan, what was the food and clothing of the Mongols like?

3. After Chinggis Khan, what was the food and clothing of the Mongols like?

4. Does Juvaini approve or disapprove of the rise and rule of the Mongols?

5. What warning did Chinggis Khan's envoy give to Zarnuq?

6. How did Zarnuq respond? What was the result?

7. What was the response of Nur? The result?

8. What, according to Juvaini, did Chinggis Khan say from a pulpit after his destruction and looting of Bukhara?

9. How did one man who escaped from Bukhara after its capture describe the fate of the city at the hands of the Mongols?

H. Wassaf

Wassaf al-Hadrat, a Persian historian, worked as a tax collector for the Mongols. His history, which covers the period 1257 to 1328, is written in an extraordinarily florid and bombastic style. An adequate English translation of his *Tarikh-i Wassaf* ("Wassaf's History") does not exist, as many scholars have shied away from the daunting task of penetrating his prose, much less translating it. The excerpt below should afford some flavor of his original Persian work.

The Ilkhan Dynasty in Persia (1256–1335/54)

Wassaf al-Hadrat

The Development Up to the Conversion of the Dynasty to Islam

The Mongol Conquest of Baghdad (1258)

Out of fear, the order was proclaimed to barricade the streets, and to station numerous troops on the walls. The two Dawādārs, the cupbearer, Suleimān Shāh and other heads of the army and the Mamluks sent, to help them, a large crowd got together from among the ordinary people of Baghdad and armed with various weapons. The next day, when the golden-winged *anka* [a miraculous bird] stretched its wings in the green nest of heaven, and the surface of the earth, after having been dark as the dwelling of the wretched, was filled with light and sound, like the heart of those who see their wishes fulfilled, the eagle standard of the Ilkhan, the bird of good fortune, proudly raised its neck from the head of fury and the fire of the fight burst forth, and the wood on which it fed was the doom of Baghdad. [. . . Arab double verse.] Inside the city it looked as though the sea were about to be smothered, or the edge of the *Thahlān* mountains to be shattered by the strength of the arm, or the sun to be covered in clay; or as though one were to flee the earthquake with a kick of the foot or to draw off the flame of the lightning and extinguish it with one's sleeve. They armed themselves for the fight and prepared the mangonels, ballistas and battering rams. The bird of arrows rose and flew from the curved-edged fortress of the bow [Koranic verse . . .] and the eagle of pain began to open its claws of fury. With the setting up of the siege tent, the large and small mangonels were brought into action and correctly conjugated right at the beginning by the efforts of those operating them, and as according to the laws of inflection the determining case is followed by the operative case, so the pointed words of the arrows were shot in answer to pre-determined questions. That day, the fight and the smoke of the battle lasted as long as the golden reined and yellow horse of the sun was made to gambol along the riding track of the heavens by the ordainer of destiny. The arrows and bolts, the lances and spears, the stones from the slings and catapults of both sides shot up to heaven at top speed like messengers of the prayer of the just, and briskly fell down like the judgment of fate. The people were killed, both from inside and outside, or were carried away wounded . . . [. . . Persian hemistich]. [Then], the Ilkhan ordered that the hand should be withdrawn from the fight. In this way was Baghdad besieged and terrorized for fifty days. But, since the city was still holding out, the order was given for the baked bricks which were lying outside the city to be collected, and from them high towers constructed in all quarters, quite close to the streets and alleys of Baghdad. On top of these they set up the catapults. The city was filled with thunder and lightning by the striking of stones and the flares from the naphtha pots; a dew of arrows rained from the cloud of bows, and the inhabitants were trampled under foot by the forces of weakness and humiliation; the cry went up: 'We have no strength today against

Goliath and his army.' The river Tigris which flows through the center of Baghdad, as the Milky Way pours through the center of heaven, was blocked on all sides and all possibility of flight was barred. On the other side the Pādishāh's fiery storming army, a heaving sea, stood guard at the post of revenge: 'Behind him hell will open and his thirst will be quenched with stinking water.' In the meantime, . . . [three Shi'ite dignitaries] . . . had, by means of a messenger, sent a letter to His Majesty Hülägü Khan, reading:

'We submit ourselves, our families and our lands, for we have knowledge passed on to us from our forebears, the twelve Imāms, and we know equally from the mouth of 'Ali, 'Ali, the prince of the true believers, the bravest among the armies, the most courageous on the seas, the bold, he who is served by pious wishes, *the friend of his friends, the enemy of his enemies,* the strongly built fast-striking one, the eloquent and bright-eyed one who trails behind him a train of riches, he who is the owner of the whirling sword, who speeds up the gifts and favors slow in coming, and with his ring unites the commandments in truth, who combines the extremes of braveness and mildness, and is the entrance gate to all knowledge, whose mercies are extensive, whose strides are long, whose wit is sharper than the . . .'s sight, who has said: *if the hidden were unveiled,* the lion of God, the mighty—from 'Alī ibn Abī Tālib's mouth we have knowledge that you will one day be the owners of this land, that the grip of your power will defeat its governor, and that he will give way before the verdict of greatness. In these words, they were referring to the following sentences of 'Alī the Pleasing (May God glorify his countenance!): "When the bond, the indissoluble comes, you will in truth be destroyed, O mother of cruelty and home of injustices, O mother of adversity. Woe to you, O Baghdad! Woe to your inhabited palaces which have wings as the wings of peacocks which will be dissolved as salt in water. There will come the sons of Kantura, and their leader of mighty voice; they have faces like leather-covered shields and noses like the trunks of elephants; they will not enter a land without conquering it, and approach no flag without overturning it."'

Hülägü who was highly pleased about this gave them presents and certificates, and sent to them Takla and 'Alā ad-Dīn, the Persian, who had been entrusted with the governorship. In this way the inhabitants of Hilla [south of Baghdad; mostly Shi'ites] put on the kaftan of security and drank from the cup of peacock friendship.

The caliph, quite secure against the internal enemies of the dynasty, against acquaintances who were less close to him than friends, against hidden enemies and open friends, against those who have had experience of gain and loss, [. . . Arab double verse] asked for means of relief in this terrible adversity and for means of averting this fearful attack: where there was a remedy for this torment and where in this general time of misfortune there was help. He wept and moaned:

'Every morning my sigh rises to the roof of heaven,
and tells the world of the smouldering heart:
The tear, teetering on the brink of the eye,
threatens, as the Tigris, to burst its banks at any moment.'

The vizier reported: The army of the Mongols is infinitely large, and there is no one present in the city who might be able to offer resistance to this enemy with chess figures. The efforts of the Mamluks and of this hastily gathered rabble are as ineffective as the *twitchings of a slaughtered animal.* By now defense against this enemy has become impossible, and his power becomes more and more overwhelming, resources and means of help are exhausted, and the people find it increasingly difficult to hold on to their courage. For the benefit of everybody and in the interest of the general welfare, it is necessary that the prince of the true believers, on the strength of the passage in the traditional writings [in the Hadīth] . . . desist from the fight with the Turks, that he may achieve salvation here for everyone, because the Turks themselves will not give up the fight, for they are *wrathful beyond measure*. It is the action of the wise, to humble themselves and to humiliate themselves; and it is a totally reasonable action, to flatter and show courtesy for the sake of the name and honour of the empire and the splendor of power [. . . two verses].

It would be best for the prince of the true believers to submit willingly and voluntarily, without argument or reservation, to the service of Hülägü Khan. The reason for the Ilkhan movements may well be greed for goods and riches; if the Caliph makes good use of this, once we have reestablished the system of good relations, we shall help ourselves and gain strength the best by means of intermarriage, and we shall make sure to lay the foundations of the means to victory, in such a way that a daughter of the Khanate shall be married to the prince of the faithful, and a pearl of the shell of the Imāmate shall be threaded onto the nuptial necklace so that, through these preparatory arrangements, empire and religion shall fuse, so that sovereignty and splendor, Caliphate and power become one, in order to save the blood and the possessions of so many thousand Muslims on earth, and so that the dignity and greatness of the Caliphate shall be magnified with the aid of the mighty Pādishāh. [Arab hemistich by the author.]

> You wish this to happen,
> However, Time says: no!

The flood of fear and horror in the Caliph's mind heaved so mightily, that truth and error remained hidden from him, and the difference between sincerity and mendacity remained obscured, since outwardly these words seemed to agree with the prophesy and the success seemed to warrant the means; and in this sentence the Caliph accepted the correctness of the second part without considering whether the first part included any error, and confirmed what the enemy had thought. Anybody who is slow-witted enough to be taken in by the deceit of the enemy deserves his evil fate, and anybody who neglects being cautious will in spite of himself lose control over affairs and sadly and dejectedly will rightly say to himself [. . . Arab verse].

In short, when it was the day of fate for al-Musta'sim [the Caliph since 1242], a day black as pitch, like the clothing of Abba's family, and his judgement followed the guide of misfortune [there follows a series of further symbolic comparisons mentioning numerous former Caliphs], he made his way on Sunday, 10 February, 1258 (4 Safar 656 H.) [Koranic verse], on a day of desperation and of faces lined with anguish, on a day unhappy for both the prominent and the common people, [Koranic verse:] 'on a day, whose evil was far spread,' with his two sons Abū Bakr and 'Abd ar-Rahmān, with a great following of Alids and learned men, of holy men of the land and trusted men of the court, with his troops and followers, with most of his pages and protected relatives, to the stirrup of the Ilkhan majesty, and amid cries of 'Look up!' he passed along the broad road of destruction, that is out from the streets of Baghdad. [. . . verse.]

When they had reached the vicinity of Rabz, . . . the crowd was prevented from entering, and only the Caliph and his sons with two or three servants were allowed to go in. Having waited for some time in the anteroom, the Caliph said to himself: [. . . Arab double verse].

Suleimān Shāh, the Dawādār and the cupbearer, together with a number of the closest confidants of the Caliph were executed by order of the Pādishāh [Hülägü]. In the morning, when the orange of Zulaikhā' [the sun] was placed at the rim of the dish of the horizon and the light by sleight of hand had conjured away from the mercury blanket of the sky the imprinted seals of the stars, the Ilkhan ordered the army to carry the torch of plunder and robbery into Baghdad. [. . Arab half verse.]

First of all they razed to the ground the walls which were mentioned in the verse of the Koran, 'Erect between yourselves and them a rampart," and filled in the moat which was as deep as the contemplation of rational men. Then, they swept through the city like hungry falcons attacking a flight of doves, or like raging wolves attacking sheep, with loose rein and shameless faces, murdering and spreading fear; [Koranic verse:] 'God leads the way to the house of salvation, and leads whom he will on to the right path.' The massacre was so great that the blood of the slain flowed in a river like the Nile, red as the wood used in dyeing, and the verse of the Koran: 'Both seed and stem perished' was recited about the goods and riches of Baghdad. With the broom of looting, they swept out the treasures from the harems of Baghdad, and with the hammer of fury, they threw down the battlements head first as if disgraced. The palaces whose canopies, on account of their ornamentation, had made the seats of paradise hide in shame and cover their shortcomings, were demolished. The verse was quoted: 'How many gardens and fountains and sown fields and splendid edifices have they not left behind' [. . . Persian double verse]. And a lament reached the ears . . . from roofs and gates: [. . . Arab verse]. The moving quill of events wrote on the leaves of the walls, and on the roofs reaching to the sky, the inscription: [. . . two verses]. Beds and cushions made of gold and encrusted with jewels were cut to pieces with knives and torn to shreds; those hidden behind the veils of the great harem [. . . Persian verse] were dragged like the hair of the idols through the streets and alleys; each of them became a plaything in the hands of a Tatar monster; and the brightness of the day became darkened for these mothers of virtues.

([Wassaf Geschichte Wassafs, ed. in Persian and trans. into German by Josef von Hammer-Purgstall, Vol. I [Vienna, 1856], pp. 68–75 =trans.pp.66 72.)

Study Questions

1. How long did the Mongols besiege Baghdad?

2. What did the Mongols do to help in their siege of Baghdad?

3. What prophecy did certain Shi'ites apparently believe?

4. With whom does Wassaf seem to identify the Mongols?

5. What was the fate of Baghdad?

I. Marco Polo

Marco Polo (1254–1324) is without a doubt the most famous Western traveller ever to venture all the way to Mongolia and China. He was born in Venice while his father and uncle, both merchants, were away on their first journey to "Cathay," or China. While in Mongolia they favorably impressed the great Khubilai, Genghis Khan's grandson and Grand Khan of the Mongol world empire since 1260. In 1271 they travelled to Mongolia and China again, this time taking with them the young Marco. Marco claims to have favorably impressed Khubilai, who (again by Marco's account) made him an envoy to several places and even appointed him governor of a Chinese province. Khubilai eventually decided reluctantly to allow the Polos to return to Venice, which they finally reached in 1295, having successfully taken with them the great wealth they had accumulated in China.

Venice and Genoa were at war in 1298, and during the course of the war Marco was captured and confined in a Genoese prison. While in prison he dictated his account of his travels to a cellmate. His account achieved popularity and has captivated generations of readers ever since. Many readers were quite skeptical of some of his claims, and he soon gained a reputation for being an exaggerator. Subsequent scholarly investigations have affirmed the truthfulness of much of his account. A recent book by librarian Frances Wood[5] attempts to cast doubt on the veracity of some of Marco's claims and descriptions, but her book has been criticized.

---

5. Frances Wood, *Did Marco Polo Go to China?* (Boulder: Westview Press, 1996).

The Travels Of Marco Polo

Chapter LII

Concerning the Customs of the Tartars

Now that we have begun to speak of the Tartars, I have plenty to tell you on that subject. The Tartar custom is to spend the winter in warm plains, where they find good pasture for their cattle, whilst in summer they betake themselves to a cool climate among the mountains and valleys, where water is to be found as well as woods and pastures.

Their houses are circular, and are made of wands covered with felts. These are carried along with them whithersoever they go; for the wands are so strongly bound together, and likewise so well combined, that the frame can be made very light. Whenever they erect these huts the door is always to the south. They also have waggons covered with black felt so efficaciously that no rain can get in. These are drawn by oxen and camels, and the women and children travel in them. The women do the buying and selling, and whatever is necessary to provide for the husband and household; for the men all lead the life of gentlemen, troubling themselves about nothing but hunting and hawking, and looking after their goshawks and falcons, unless it be the practice of warlike exercises.

They live on the milk and meat which their herds supply, and on the produce of the chase; and they eat all kinds of flesh, including that of horses and dogs, and Pharaoh's rats, of which last there are great numbers in burrows on those plains. Their drink is mare's milk.

They are very careful not to meddle with each other's wives, and will not do so on any account, holding that to be an evil and abominable thing. The women too are very good and loyal to their husbands, and notable housewives withal. [Ten or twenty of them will dwell together in charming peace and unity, nor shall you ever hear an ill word among them.]

The marriage customs of Tartars are as follows. Any man may take a hundred wives as he so please, and if he be able to keep them. But the first wife is ever held most in honour, and as the most legitimate [and the same applies to the sons whom she may bear]. The husband gives a marriage payment to his wife's mother, and the wife brings nothing to her husband. They have more children than other people, because they have so many wives. They may marry their cousins, and if a father dies, his son may take any of the wives, his own mother always excepted; that is to say the eldest son may do this, but no other. A man may also take the wife of his own brother after the latter's death. Their weddings are celebrated with great ado.

Chapter LIII

Concerning the God of the Tartars

This is the fashion of their religion. [They say there is a Most High God of Heaven, whom they worship daily with thurible and incense, but they pray to Him only for health of mind and body. But] they have [also] a certain [other] god of theirs called *Natigay,* and they say he is the god of the Earth, who watches over their children, cattle, and crops. They show him great worship and honour, and every man hath a figure of him in his house, made of felt and cloth; and they also make in the same manner images of his wife and children. The wife they put on the left hand, and the children in front. And when they eat, they take the fat of the meat and grease the god's mouth withal, as well as the mouths of his wife and children. Then they take of the broth and sprinkle it before the door of the house; and that done, they deem that their god and his family have had their share of the dinner.

Their drink is mare's milk, prepared in such a way that you would take it for white wine; and a right good drink it is, called by them *Kemiz.*

The clothes of the wealthy Tartars are for the most part of gold and silk stuffs, lined with costly furs, such as sable and ermine, vair and fox-skin, in the richest fashion.

Chapter LIV

Concerning the Tartar Customs of War

All their harness of war is excellent and costly. Their arms are bows and arrows, sword and mace; but above all the bow, for they are capital archers, indeed the best that are known. On their backs they wear armour of cuirbouly, prepared from buffalo and other hides, which is very strong. They are excellent soldiers, and passing valiant in battle. They are also more capable of hardships than other nations; for many a time, if need be, they will go for a month without any supply of food, living only on the milk of their mares and on such game as their bows may win them. Their horses also will subsist entirely on the grass of the plains, so that there is no need to carry store of barley or straw or oats; and they are very docile to their riders. These, in case of need, will abide on horseback the livelong night, armed at all points, while the horse will be continually grazing.

Of all troops in the world these are they which endure the greatest hardship and fatigue, and which cost the least; and they are the best of all for making wide conquests of country. And this you will perceive from what you have heard and shall hear in this book; and (as a fact) there can be no manner of doubt that now they are the masters of the biggest half of the world. Their troops are admirably ordered in the manner that I shall now relate.

You see, when a Tartar prince goes forth to war, he takes with him, say, 100,000 horse. Well, he appoints an officer to every ten men, one to every hundred, one to every thousand, and one to every ten thousand, so that his own orders have to be given to ten persons only, and each of these ten persons has to pass the orders only to other ten, and so on; no one having to give orders to more than ten. And every one in turn is responsible only to the officer immediately over him; and the discipline and order that comes of this method is marvellous, for they are a people very obedient to their chiefs. Further, they call the corps of 100,000 men a *Tuc*; that of 10,000 they call *a Toman*; the thousand they call; . . . the hundred *Guz*; the ten . . . And when the army is on the march they have always 200 horsemen, very well mounted, who are sent a distance of two marches in advance to reconnoitre, and these always keep ahead. They have a similar party detached in the rear, and on either flank, so that there is a good look-out kept on all sides against a surprise. When they are going on a distant expedition they take no gear with them except two leather bottles for milk; a little earthenware pot to cook their meat in, and a little tent to shelter them from rain. And in case of great urgency they will ride ten days on end without lighting a fire or taking a meal. On such an occasion they will sustain themselves on the blood of their horses, opening a vein and letting the blood jet into their mouths drinking till they have had enough, and then staunching it.

They also have milk dried into a kind of paste to carry with them; and when they need food they put this in water, and beat it up till it dissolves, and then drink it. [It is prepared in this way; they boil the milk, and when the rich part floats on the top they skim it into another vessel, and of that they make butter; for the milk will not become solid till this is removed. Then they put the milk in the sun to dry. And when they go on an expedition, every man takes some ten pounds of this dried milk with him. And of a morning he will take a half pound of it and put it in his leather bottle, with as much water as he pleases. So, as he rides along, the milk-paste and the water in the bottle get well churned together into a kind of pap, and that makes his dinner.]

When they come to an engagement with the enemy, they will gain the victory in this fashion. [They never let themselves get into a regular medley, but keep perpetually riding round and shooting into the enemy. And] as they do not count it any shame to run away in battle, they will [sometimes pretend to] do so, and in running away they turn in the saddle and shoot hard and strong at the foe, and in this way make great havoc. Their horses are trained so perfectly that they will double hither and thither, just like a dog, in a way that is quite astonishing. Thus they fight to as good purpose in running away as if they stood and faced the enemy, because of the vast volleys of arrows that they shoot in this way, turning round upon their pursuers, who are fancying that they have won the battle. But when the Tartars see that they have killed and wounded a good many horses and men, they wheel round bodily, and return to the charge in perfect order and with loud cries; and in a very short time the enemy are routed In truth they are stout and valiant soldiers, and inured to war. And you perceive that it is just when the enemy sees them run, and imagines that he has gained the battle, that he has in reality lost it; for the Tartars wheel round in a moment when they judge the right time has come. And after this fashion they have won many a fight.

All this that I have been telling you is true of the manners and customs of the genuine Tartars. But I must add also that in these days they are greatly degenerated; for those who are settled in Cathay have taken up the practices of the Idolaters of the country, and have abandoned their own institutions; whilst those who have settled in the Levant have adopted the customs of the Saracens.

Chapter LV
Concerning the Administering of Justice Among the Tartars

The way they administer justice is this. When any one has committed a petty theft, they give him, under the orders of authority, seven blows of a stick, or seventeen, or twenty-seven, or thirty-seven, or forty-seven, and so forth, always increasing by tens in proportion to the injury done, and running up to one hundred and seven. Of these beatings sometimes they die. But if the offence be horse-stealing, or some other great matter, they cut the thief in two with a sword. Howbeit, if he be able to ransom himself by paying nine times the value of the thing stolen, he is let off. Every Lord or other person who possesses beasts has them marked with his peculiar brand, be they horses, mares, camels, oxen, cows, or other great cattle, and then they are sent abroad to graze over the plains without any keeper. They get all mixt together, but eventually every beast is recovered by means of its owner's brand, which is known. For their sheep and goats they have shepherds. All their cattle are remarkably fine, big, and in good condition.

They have another notable custom, which is this. If any man have a daughter who dies before marriage, and another man have had a son also die before marriage, the parents of the two arrange a grand wedding between the dead lad and lass. And marry them they do, making a regular contract! And when the contract papers are made out they put them in the fire, in order (as they will have it) that the parties in the other world may know the fact, and so look on each other as man and wife. And the parents thenceforward consider themselves sib to each other, just as if their children had lived and married. Whatever may be agreed on between the parties as dowry, those who have to pay it cause to be painted on pieces of paper and then put these in the fire, saying that in that way the dead person will get all the real articles in the other world.

Study Questions

1. According to Marco Polo, how did the "Tartars" move about over the course of a year?

2. How did Marco Polo describe the Mongols' houses?

3. What was the food and drink of the Mongols?

4. According to Marco Polo, did the Mongols frequently commit adultery?

5. What did Marco say about "kemiz"?

6. What did Marco say about the physical endurance of Mongolian mounted archers?

7. How was the Mongolian army organized?

8. In cases of "great urgency," how did Mongolian mounted archers sustain themselves?

9. How did Mongolian mounted archers make milk on their expeditions?

10. What were some Mongolian strategies in warfare?

11. What were Mongolian punishments for petty thievery?

12. How did owners of livestock distinguish their criminals from those owned by others?